for our good neighbors!

Alfred

May '01

The Rewards of
PARENTING

Growing along with your child

The Rewards of
PARENTING
Growing along with your child

Alfred J.R. Koumans *M.D., M.T.S.*

Rutledge Books, Inc.   Danbury, CT

Rutledge Books, Inc.
107 Mill Plain Road
Danbury, CT 06811
1-800-278-8533
www.rutledgebooks.com

Manufactured in the United States of America

Cataloging in Publication Data
    Koumans, Alfred J.R.
    The Rewards of Parenting: Growing along with your child

    ISBN: 1-58244-101-4

    1. Parenting. 2. Parent-Child Relationship. 3. Family Roles

Library of Congress Card Number: 00-109270

Authors, when lucky, have a host of unseen helpmates: all those whose ideas and support have aided and encouraged them.

It is my wife Jeltje, the muse of this book, who I credit with the impetus to do something creative with my thoughts about children's influence on their parents. Our children Emily, Marnix and Josephine have been a continuing inspiration for writing it.

I am also grateful for the unfailing interest and support of my good friends William Crout, Frank Formica and Carl Scovel. They enlivened for years the lonely work of writing.

Of the many sympathisers with this project, Roy Schulte stood out with his comments and vignettes.

For their effort and contributions in the early stages of this project I acknowledge a debt to Cyrisse Jaffee, Judy Kaplan, Ken Rivard, Larry Rothstein and Pam Suma.

My editor and the staff at Rutledge Books, Inc. stood ready with their patience and expertise to correct, edit and transform a manuscript into this publication.

(The vignettes in the text come from experiences with my own and friends' children, acquaintances, relatives, patients and those already mentioned above. To ensure confidentiality identifying data have been changed and recast.)

CONTENTS

INTRODUCTION

When a father gives to his son, both laugh;
when a son gives to his father, both cry.
Yiddish Proverb

One summer afternoon almost thirty years ago, I was walking through the Vermont woods with my five-year-old daughter, Josy, and her eight-year-old brother, Mark. My wife and I had taken to camping in the wilds as an antidote to our city and work routines. Together we explored the world.

The children and I pushed through the trees into a clearing and came upon a mountain stream. "Look, Daddy," Josy cried, "water is coming out of the rock!"

She pointed to a large boulder over which water was flowing in a glistening film. The boulder was smooth except for a barely visible ridge, halfway down, where the water fanned out in a spray of droplets.

I was about to explain, "No, dear, the water's not coming out of the rock. It's actually coming from above and when it hits the ridge it looks like it's coming out of the rock." I could have taken her tiny fingers and touched the stream as it flowed downward to prove it.

Something compelled me to keep silent. She knew that water wasn't supposed to come out of a rock, but why spoil a perfectly good miracle? I just stood quietly by, sharing in her pleasure at our discovery.

After a few minutes, we got underway again. Josy and Mark led the way up the trail. A short hike brought us to an abandoned logging road, where we came upon a young maple with an oddly deformed trunk. The trunk grew straight up from its base, but at the shoulder height it made a right angle for a few inches, then bent upright again. We stopped to look at it. I wondered privately why the tree had grown that way—had it been twisted by a storm? Suffered a childhood trauma? With Josy's miraculous stream still fresh in my mind, I now turned to Mark. "What do you think?" I asked.

"Maybe it has crooked roots," he answered matter-of-factly.

I laughed. Instead of my arid, analytical explanation, my son had come up with a richer and more inclusive answer. His response filled me with delight, even if it was, like Josy's, scientifically inaccurate. Most parents, if open to the experience, can attest to the power of an unexpected utterance by their children to refresh their world, to see it as a place of miracles, where water comes out of rocks and where what exists above ground is only a mirror image of its magical subterranean counterpart. Part of me had gotten lost in the grind of my work. I had lost my sense of wonder and openness to the possibilities of life. This was the source of my impulse to check my rational explanations. In retrospect, I believe that countless of like experiences with my children inoculated me against taking myself too seriously, against becoming the omniscient psychiatrist who values his opinions to the exclusion of those of his patients'. These experiences reminded me of the limits of one's own vision.

Incidents like these are valuable in their own right, but something else seemed to be going on. For some reason I felt that a vital question had found its fitting answer.

Weeks later, I was still thinking about that afternoon in the country. The more I thought about it, the clearer it became why I had felt so moved by my children's observations. I had been "primed" for them. I was at a developmental crossroads in my life, searching and uncertain. My children had provided me with just the sort of spark I needed to go on.

For the previous ten years I had been busy establishing my family. We lived in our first house and the children liked their school. Even our social life was beginning to pick up after a period of benign neglect in the first years of parenthood. My wife was embarking on her career and mine was firmly settled. After all the years of sitting at the feet of masters, study and taking exams, I now found myself teaching the residents at a hospital and publishing papers. The years of receiving and absorbing had given way to a period of providing and producing, for my children, for the next generation of doctors, and for my patients.

We had just arrived at a comfort zone after adapting to a new country and building our lives. A breathing space was opening up. The years ahead appeared predictable; the pace manageable; the direction set.

Just at that point I remember feeling at times tempted to settle in snug comfort and let the future take care of itself. But intuition warned me that this road would lead to a smug routine and a respectable professional and physical paunch. I knew I had to keep the pot stirred to keep the years ahead ripe with potential and change. What I needed was a built-in element of surprise and renewal to guard against incipient stagnation. But how?

We rarely intuit these needs of our own personal development with definitive clarity. We grope for it. In my case it showed up occasionally in my irritation at the status quo in a search for variety in life. We found ourselves looking at camping equipment. The five of us embarked on vacations that contrasted with our daily routines: primitive camping in New England on weekends and vacations in the tropics or Europe. It helped, but that also could become a set pattern of its own.

The experience in the Vermont woods was a fountainhead for me, professionally and personally. It turned me around. I did not have to have all the answers or be the authority. I could gain by listening to my children and allowing them more of a say in who I was to become. As we were raising them and they grew up, I would keep growing with them. It remains for me a vivid reminder of a child's potential for helping adults through developmental transitions. I had been sensitized to my children as being a surprising source of gains for parenthood.

Parenthood provides us with a unique opportunity for psychological growth. We all grew up with the notion that parents affect their children's development. Yet most parents I have spoken with have experienced the powerful influence their children can have on them through a child's unexpectedly accurate observation, a different way of dealing with a problem, or a spontaneous expression of love. In so many ways, children affect *our* development, providing us with insights, lessons, and epiphanies. Our children can help free us from stalemated patterns of thinking, acting, and feeling; provide us with novel strategies for dealing with our psychological hang-ups; allow us to resolve problems from our past (especially with parents and siblings); and illuminate current relationships. This book will give examples of all of these, and more.

Growing up together can be a truly *collaborative* process. As we guide our kids through the developmental stages of childhood, their influence nudges us along the path through our own maturity as adults. In order to fully realize this psychological interplay, children need to be taken seriously and respected, parents need to be open to the "otherness" of their children, their observations and insights. Power needs to be shared as time goes on. When children come to feel that they matter and their opinions are appreciated, as evidenced by the role their parents let them play in their lives and their development, an atmosphere of mutuality and respect develops. Conflict, anger, rebellion, and emotional distance are less necessary. Thus, while we maximize our children's developmental progress, we gain in our own as well.

This effect of children on their parents has not been a focus in childrearing books. From Benjamin Spock to Penelope Leach and T. Berry Brazelton, parents have had many resources to help them understand and guide their children's development and tend to their daily care. Some books even provide instructions on how to meet the challenges of parenthood, while others sing its praises in a more general way. Elin Schoen's *Growing With Your Child* is an example. I know of no book that describes the personal gains for parents by alerting them to their own development, which goes on a parallel track with that of their children and shows in detail how parents have benefited by their child's input.

I believe this is the first such book. The effects of children on us (child-effects) contain a profoundly affirmative message for both generations: *in our relation with children, we can find the optimal potential for our own growth and renewal, as well as for theirs.*

Unlike the bonds we form with spouses, lovers, or friends, the one we form with our children is unique. It is the one most likely to endure. We don't select our children among others—the bond is non-elective. We have a responsibility for them no other relation shares. They are our own flesh and blood. We identify with them as with no one else. They carry us into the future beyond our own life. It is for them that we risk our lives with the greatest ease. A soldier abroad wrote to his mother: "If I kill anyone over here, will that change anything between us?" She replied, "Nothing you do will ever make me not love you. I am your mother."[i] This unique bond is powerful. It can provide us with the motivation for major change. Instead of pitting our aspirations for personal fulfillment against our obligations as parents, this bond can transform even the most commonplace aspects of parenthood into opportunities for us to grow and be regenerated.

The Rewards of Parenting is intended to be a guidebook to help you and your family along your adult developmental journey, no matter what developmental "stage" you or your child are in. Like other guidebooks, it describes the places where others have been and what they recommend or want you to avoid. It is not a "how-to" book. You choose your own itinerary. People are too different in taste, preference, and style to fit into a few simple cookbook recipes.

Comparing where you are with your child, with some of the examples that I will give you, will help you find the way to a more enjoyable and effective parenthood. It can be a major growth period in your adult life, thanks to your children. Like my moments in the forest with my kids, you may be refreshed and enlightened, discovering a new sense of self and relatedness that can so easily get lost in the chaos and stress of childrearing.

CHAPTER ONE

PARENTS AND CHILDREN:
THE WAY THEIR LIVES TOUCH

> *Maximum debetur puero reverentia*
> *(We owe the greatest respect to a child)*[ii]

We have all learned that children with their relentless growth, traverse a series of "stages" before they reach adulthood. Adults, and their inevitable decline, have only fairly recently been thought of as having their own developmental challenges to meet. Maturity is a process. Adulthood comes with growing pains, too. The changes throughout adulthood can been seen as a series of events or stages that are somewhat predictable, whether it is from leading a single, career-oriented life, to marriage and childrearing, or a reassessment in mid-life that can lead to more or less dramatic shifts as was first outlined by C.G. Jung.[iii]

On our way through the developmental changes in adulthood, our feelings, memories and thoughts can get stirred up. Unresolved problems from an earlier period can arise, and new questions need to be faced, such as changes in self-image as we get older. When we successfully master these hurdles, we gain a sense of competence and integrity, which is a concept from Erikson[iv]. Although childbearing and childrearing are themselves formidable developmental tasks for any adult, the message of this book is that the influence of our children can ease some struggles and clear up some confusions that accompany adult growing. Openness to that influence helps us to meet the challenges of adulthood more effectively.

In what ways do children effect their parents' growth and change? How does that come about? What do we need to benefit both generations? In this chapter, I explore these questions and try to formulate some answers.

Some of these child-effects are obvious. They are the result of the child being there and growing up. Anticipating a child's birth is an upheaval like a tectonic plate shift in many parents' lives. After the initial burst of elation and excitement wears off, many parents are surprised by the next wave of emotions. Some feel anxious or become superstitious. Others turn into frugal worriers or indulge in the "before it is too late," theory. Life, as they know it, is about to end, and a new, yet unknown kind of living is around the corner. Can we still do the things we have grown accustomed to? Can we cope? About-to-be parents feel the impact of the new life well before it is born.

A young woman doubted she would be capable of becoming a mother. The following is how she felt the impact of her pregnancy:

Cindy had chronic asthma since she was sixteen. She was determined to overcome the restrictions of her illness. She married at twenty-seven, held on to a good job, and had many friends. Yet she had to limit some of her activities, did not always feel well enough, felt isolated from her peers, and was frustrated in her more ambitious professional goals. Cindy was delighted when she became pregnant at age thirty. It was a difficult pregnancy and she had to take her medications for asthma. Would her body ever function normally? Instead of seeing herself as a woman with a future, she often felt like a seventy-five-year-old invalid.

However, the delivery went well and she had a healthy boy. This joyous outcome made Cindy feel, for the first time in many years, healthy and whole. Knowing she had brought forth life helped her settle some of the doubt that her chronic illness had caused. Newly confident about what she could do, Cindy felt she had overcome a major obstacle. She was now the mother of a healthy child. Now she could go on with her life, despite her illness.

Many parents are already aware of the practical ways in which the arrival of a child will change their lives. A baby not only alters your mobility, daily routines, budget, and functions of your house, but your emotions as well. No other event in life has such a radical impact—it shakes our very roots. The new life we helped create and our new responsibilities, recast our outlook on the world and ourselves. Call it a "Copernican shift." We are no longer the center of our universe. From now on there will be someone who matters more to us than we do to ourselves. For who else would we run into a burning house without even a thought? We see the world in the new light of the child's interest and beyond our own. We have found a new lodestar; an extension beyond ourselves. With it, we acquire a new identity altogether, that of "parent."

This transformation creates that unique bond between child and parent which allows their interaction to become endowed with power and meaning.

Watch how a young father, himself abused as a child, bonds with his daughter and heals his own impulsiveness:

Phil, a mechanic, was a moody and at times, impulsive man, who had left one job after a fight. But when Phil's wife told him that she was expecting their first child, this somewhat withdrawn expectant father felt ready for the task.

Phil had endured a difficult childhood. His alcoholic mother had died when he was in the second grade. His father, a traveling salesman, was an abusive man who never remarried. Since he was frequently away form home, Phil's grandmother and aunts raised him and his younger brother. He had to learn early to help take care of his younger brother and put aside many things a kid ordinarily can enjoy.

He married early. His wife depended on his competence, especially after Eve was born. They shared the burdens and tasks of childrearing evenly. Phil left his union job to freelance and his wife continued her secretarial temp work.

Soothing the crying baby in the middle of the night, diapering, feeding, tending to Eve's illnesses and even setting limits, gave Phil intense satisfaction. He was able to give what he had only sporadically and unevenly received as a child himself: the consistent attention and care of a devoted parent.

Later, when Eve was three years old, he would say, "When I do things with her, I seem to remember wanting the same things when I was a kid myself. Doing it with her makes both of us feel good now." Phil not only basked in the affection and responsive growth of his little daughter, he evidently had an inkling of how their life together was healing him. "I remember how my mother would hit me at times, but I just hold Eve when she has a tantrum until she quiets down, and then I can talk to her."

Phil learned to tame his own impulsiveness. He began to grow into a confident and jovial man.

People observing young parents have seen changes like this. But what would it have taken, you could ask, to bring about such astounding growth in a young adult? How many years of psychotherapy? It was the growing with a child that enabled him to transform himself. What kind of interaction makes this possible?

Our children send us messages in many subtle ways; messages that can influence us. Many parents are aware of these "child-effects." Some arise out of the predictable developmental changes of childhood. By this I mean both physical changes, such as teething, walking, sexual maturation, etc., and psychological ones, such as speech, understanding the world, independence, altruism, etc.

Other child-effects emerge from an interplay between parent and child. We will see examples of these, such as probing questions from the child, insightful observations, or the way the child comes to terms with a problem. Any of these can resonate with us and lead to a surprising insight on our part and in turn may move us to bring about a change in ourselves.

Even when the implications of a child's behavior are less immediately clear and need some careful deciphering for understanding, the child-effect can be just as powerful.

How we receive a child's influence, recognize and then respond to it, determines how much parent and child will gain. If we want the interplay with the child to have this beneficial effect, it will help us to know how to recognize the different ways in which our children can influence us. Once you have identified the right influences you will experience as a parent, you can begin to practice how best to respond. The parents described in this book will be the ones giving a range of examples to choose from.

To help you recognize these effects among the zillions of daily interactions with your child, I have sorted them into three categories.They are clearly defined groups of child-parent interactions.

THREE WAYS PARENTS CAN GET THE MESSAGE:

I think it will be useful for our purpose, to distinguish three ways that children have to influence their parents. I have called them: signals, symbols and sequences. Each comes with a different kind of child-parent interaction.

Signals are inevitable. They happen when your child passes the signposts of child development. Each one challenges you to a new pattern of interaction with the child. Signals can evoke strong emotional reactions and an opportunity to explore unresolved problems. *Cindy's, on page 2, was a signal.*

Symbols are less obvious messages. They are the result of some interplay between your child and you. It is often something your child will do or say when you are doing something together. Your child comments on something in words or actions when you get dressed, fix a meal, play, explain something, or set a limit—anything short of an elaborate interaction. This requires you to make an effort to interpret what was said or done to get the full message and access the full force of the symbol. Phil gained by signals and symbols.

Finally, the more elaborate series of messages we get from our children, I have called *Sequences*. They can be a conversation or expressed in an easy to interpret series of actions. Sequences happen when you and your child engage in an open interaction. They enable you to reflect on your behavior, style, or personality. Sequences are often rich in insight, providing a prime opportunity for parents to use the child's uncanny candor and perceptiveness. With this help, parents can make modification in their lives or themselves. The epiphanies I received through my children were due to sequences.

How much can you gain from these messages? It depends on who we are or what mood we are in. A poorly perceptive parent can learn simply to acknowledge the child's input rather than dismiss or ignore it. The more receptive parent will reflect on the feelings, memories and thoughts that arise. Such a parent often arrives at some interesting observation or insight. A very receptive parent is willing to do the homework and respond to the interaction with the child, re-experience some old feelings, reflect on them, let other memories or thoughts come up, and come to a new understanding. This process can bring about a new awareness, a new behavior, and a change that feels right.

The following is a more detailed description of signals, symbols and sequences at different levels of receptivity of the parent. (For those of you interested in diagrams, there is one outlining the discussion on page 24).

SIGNALS

As children grow, we become aware of several predictable stages in their development. The transition from newborn to toddler, from school-age child to adolescent and beyond, are all marked by events, some large and some small. Look! The tooth is coming through! She can walk! Grandma called, and Timmy had his first chat with her! Each of these events can be a signal that a change is taking place for your child and you.

All parents get these signals. They come with the territory. Signals are most evident as children pass the typical developmental milestones—those crucial "firsts" and "lasts" that mark a child's growth. These are first steps, first words, potty training, first day of kindergarten, first sleepover, first trip alone, the last summer before college, the last holiday dinner together before marriage, etc. But many signals are less dramatic. The first few years of your child's life are filled with firsts; all potential signals. Some are mundane activities of parenting, such as taking the child for a haircut, a first swim in the pool, a first walk to school along, a driving lesson, a date, etc. Early developmental stages are predictable. Less predictable are your feelings as your child takes these steps.

Adult development is not nearly as orderly as a child's, yet there are a series of inevitable thresholds that most adults will have to cross as they get older. Marriage, parenthood, death of a parent, retirement, illness, grandparenthood are only a few of them. As your child develops, you, as the parent, are moving on a parallel track through your own growth process. As you guide your child through one stage after the next, their marking events may stir up old feelings and even conflicts around similar transitions left over from your childhood. Memories, old feelings and associations to your own childhood experiences give the emotional charge of the signal.

Look at what one father gained from the signal "coming to terms with a sibling." This is what one father got from his child and how he dealt with it.

Frank was apprehensive when he brought three-year-old Andy to the room where Helen, his wife, was nursing their newborn. Frank and Helen had prepared Andy for this event, had let him feel the swelling tummy, shown him the bassinet, and talked about a new brother or sister. Frank, however, felt excitement mixed with a dread he could not account for right away. He managed to hold himself back as he walked hand in hand with Andy to the bed.

He just watched his little son, who, filled with eager curiosity, crawled up to the baby and touched it. "You can stroke her; it's alright," encouraged Helen, making room for him next to her. Andy held the baby's tiny hand in his. At that point, Frank became aware of a fear that his son might squeeze too hard or otherwise hurt her. Again he restrained himself and nothing happened. Andy was fascinated.

Frank noticed the difference between his son's reaction and his own. What was he afraid of and why? Why would Little Andy want to hurt his sister? Then he remembered having to call his brother with the good news. His brother, whom he had "forgotten" to call after Andy's birth. His brother, who had been married eight years and was childless. The brother he had always been compared to by his parents, not always favorably. "Why don't you pick up your room the way your brother does?" This brother whom he had fought with way too often when they were children and who now lived far away. His younger brother…yes! That was it!

He could not image that Andy actually might like a little sister more than being envious. He watched as Andy tenderly stroked the downy little head. It was his problem, not Andy's; his old envy of his brother, the anger, and their battles. Frank began to feel amazed, strangely reassured and relieved.

Later he talked it over with Helen. He kept watching his reactions as their two children grew up. He and Helen avoided making the hurtful comparisons between their two children that his own parents had burdened him with. They appreciated each child for their own gifts and qualities. The children had little sibling rivalry and became close, and stayed close even as young adults.

Frank had become a better parent. He could also begin to make belated amends to his brother.

This father's restraint during his son's first encounter with a sibling made it possible for him to see how his boy dealt with it. The difference between his son and him was an eye-opener. He did his homework. He did or said nothing to even suggest that there could be anger or envy, which had been his problem. Later he acknowledged that it really was his little boy's unexpected tenderness towards his new sister that triggered his self-examination and prodded him to change his attitude.

Frank responded to the signal on a very perceptive level. At a less perceptive level, he could have thought back on his own childhood experience of coming to terms with his younger brother and leave it at that. At the "the least" perceptive level, he might have given in to this impulse to restrain Andy and warn him "not to squeeze too hard," and continue to expect signs of sibling rivalry. If his children had sensed that (as often they do), they might have come to believe it was expected and act accordingly.

Caring for and living with a newborn produces a variety of signals, which can be the start of a series of significant opportunities for insight and growth. Having a child invites us daily to consider what style of parenting we prefer, and what our goals and values will be. It leads us to reflect on our own upbringing and our relationship with our parents.

Becoming a parent is a signal for changing the relationship with our own parents.

Jane and Bob had noticed, during the infrequent visits of their parents to their home, that the folks had been gushing about the babies and toddlers. They had four in all, but when they became preschoolers and showed more of a personality of their own, the two sets of grandparents were sometimes taken aback by what the kids said or did. Since the four of them were a happy bunch, had nice playmates, did not get into trouble, were generally cooperative and fun, they had decided not to discuss their parents' growing displeasure with them.

One day when all four grandparents happened to be in town and visiting, Jane and Bob found themselves facing a tribunal of four solemn judges. Jane's father read the verdict: "We don't want you both to be upset or feel criticized in any way. We love your children more than we can say. But we agree that we are concerned about the way they are growing up." Jane and her husband were put on edge. "What do you mean?" The answer came from her mother: "Well, dear, it's small things really. But we fear that unless you do something about it now, your kids will be in trouble when they get older."

It turned out that both sets of grandparents had been put off by the "lack of manners" from their grandchildren. They did not behave as expected. They did not always greet their grandparents when they came down for breakfast or back from preschool. They were not respectful. They would not always do what they were told, etc. This, of course, would lead to social difficulties of all kinds later in life, and God knows how difficult it already was.

Fortunately, Jane and her husband had anticipated some of this. They could hold their ground in good spirit and simply tell their parents that yes, their kids had not been "trained" exactly like they had been. Ideas about childrearing had changed quite a bit. They, too, valued manners and social graces, but wanted to focus on other aspects of growing up first, such as getting along with each other and peers, and getting a sense of themselves. They would prefer the kids to behave not with a learned reflex, but from a sense of respect for the other person. Perhaps, if the grandparents could be less covertly critical, the kids would respond and become more sensitive to them and what they valued so much.

The tribunal was speechless and adjourned. Life went on and the kids did great. After fifteen year, the then surviving grandparents apologized to Jane and Bob for what they must have put them through that day, and admitted how mistaken they had been.

Jane and Bob had to confront their own parents on the point of parenthood. This is a quite common situation as the generations follow each other up and become aware of their differences. It was, in a way, a capstone on their emancipation from youth. Having to account for how they raised the children, they clearly and irrevocably set a boundary between the generations. "These are our kids and our responsibility. We will listen to your opinions, but don't expect us to always agree with them."

Signals start with the birth of the child and never stop,

although they may become less frequent as the rate of developmental change slows down. Once we can recognize their quality as marking a new stage in the child's life, we begin to feel more comfortable in exploring our reaction to the event. What happens if we are reluctant or unable to acknowledge a problem caused by a signal and can make no sense of our feelings? In that case we are stuck and continue to react without thinking. We have deprived ourselves of an opportunity for change or growth.

Not each signal will necessarily produce a Hollywood-style flash of ready-made insight or a quick solution to a vexing problem. In the first few years of your child's life there are too many signals to pursue the meaning of, but if we cultivate an alertness to them and learn how to read them, we can feel more comfortable with parenting and with our own developmental journey from marital partner through parenthood to, perhaps, grandparenthood. The insights we gain on the way and the changes they inspire can be applied to other partnerships in life: marriage, co-workers, friendships, and aging parents. We saw this already in the cases of Cindy, Phil and Frank, and more examples will follow.

SYMBOLS

When a child's message is not as straightforward as a signal, it remains a symbol, needing some interpretation before we can understand and absorb it. A child's influence frequently finds symbolic expression, even in well-functioning families.

There are many reasons why children's efforts to get through to us become a symbol instead of a sequence. Some reasons may have to do with the child, but we will not go into those here. Parents may be too tired, preoccupied or inexperienced to recognized a symbol or help create a sequence. It can sometimes be really embarrassing to hear a child's candid observation or notice "Junior" meeting a challenge we had trouble with ourselves.

Parents of six-year-old Tommy sat down after dinner to communicate. Mother, the communicator, had decided something had to be settled between them. They believed that Tommy had gone to bed. As their conversation gained speed and volume, the mother seemed to have more to say and the father less and less. Her voice rose, and his sank. There was anger in the air. Suddenly they heard a little voice coming from the second floor landing: "How can you have a discussion if Mom is doing all the talking?"

After a silence, Mother turned to Father, bent forward and said calmly, "Could you please take that knife out of my back?" Yet she credits, years later, Tommy's intervention with a more even-handed style of discussing things with her husband (and others).

Instead of welcoming such an input, we may be tempted to respond by belittling it or refusing to notice. Often we limit our interactions with our children because we look at kids as needing guidance, not providing it. Historically and culturally, children have rarely been taken seriously and their contribution to us was considered trivial.

Many parents, even today, were raised without having a voice that counted in the household. It may be difficult not to copy what we grew up with, but establish a more accepting attitude and take our child seriously, even if it embarrasses us or tweaks our pride. To encourage children's influence, we must also be willing to gradually share power in decisions that directly affect them. This helps to avoid the control battles that some parents find themselves caught in later. Encouraging and valuing our children's contributions helps us solve our own developmental dilemmas. It makes for a healthy family dynamic.

Unless we make this conscious effort, our parenting style will be largely limited by our own experience of being brought up. We then often end up imitating our parents or doing the opposite as a rejection of them. The result of these adopted agendas can easily be a limitation of our children's interaction with us. The price for this is less rewards of parenting.

If we don't take our children's communications seriously, they may end up feeling that their contributions don't count for much or are not welcome. They shut up or "turn up the volume," act up in troublesome ways, or wholly disguise what they mean. What they feel will still emerge somehow, but often disguised in such a way that the child is less at risk. Just to pick a few examples: excessive desire to please, trouble at school, moodiness, obstreperousness, can all be disguises for their messages. These can all be symbols waiting for a sensitive ear.

Of course, when our children have to speak in riddles or act in symbols if they don't want to be disregarded or put down, we run the chance of misinterpreting the symbol or missing the message altogether. The hidden message of a symbol is the key to its benefit.

Let us look at an example from real life:

Mr. Brown ran a summer camp for emotionally disturbed kids. It had an excellent reputation and many campers returned year after year. For him, they were simply "my kids." Besides the usual summer camp activities, there was counseling with an emphasis on role models and following examples.

Among the kids was Eddy, a scrawny, shy, mildly retarded boy who seemed to have found a safe place under Mr. Brown's wings. He quietly took part in the activities, but came to life wen he could assist with simple office tasks in Mr. Brown's office. After a few years of this, he even managed some degree of responsibility: sorting the mail, making phone calls for deliveries, etc.

One summer, someone mentioned to Mr. Brown that Eddy showed cranky moods: raising his voice, a frown on his face, and an occasional four-letter word. "That's not Eddy," said the informant. Mr. Brown agreed and promised to watch him. It was a particularly tight summer with budget problems, sicknesses, and bad weather. Even Mr. Brown had a hard time remaining cool and collected, especially with the calls from long-winded, demanding parents who rarely visited.

It was not until he watched one day how Eddy barked into his phone and slammed it down, that he realized how bad it had become. He cradled his head in his hands, closed his eyes and just sat at his desk, remembering how yesterday he had lost his temper and slammed down the phone himself. And that was not the only time. Eddy, sitting around the corner at his own little desk, must have seen him. *Damn! What an example!*

Instead of taking Eddy to task for his unbecoming behavior, Mr. Brown had a quiet talk with Eddy and made sure that he found other ways of dealing with his own frustration. Pretty soon Eddy was back to his usual self, but Mr. Brown was not. When he told me this anecdote a few years later, he added, "I have never since slammed down the phone. I have become much more careful with how I behave under stress, certainly when others are around. I have to learn a few more tricks, but what a difference it makes!"

Eddy was not Mr. Brown's child, but Mr. Brown acted *in loco parentis* (in the parental role) and was subject to the same child-effects as parents can be. By accepting the notion that Eddy's behavior was a symbol of something else, Mr. Brown already had a minimum benefit from this kind of effect. He had realized that his behavior was serious enough to have an affect on Eddy, and that Eddy was copying him. If he had only sat down and chided Eddy, acknowledging the office tensions both of them were under, he would have had a moderate benefit. However, Mr. Brown went for the gold when his concern about Eddy's outburst encouraged him to moderate his own tensions and become more even-tempered. This was a maximum benefit.

Life abounds in examples of symbols, as does literature and movies. It is probably the most frequent interaction of any interest to parents. In the movie *On Golden Pond,* a not-so-innocent grandson reacquaints his irascible grandfather with the meaning of love and family. That grandfather is then able, for the first and last time, to let his daughter know that he loves and approves of her. In Lucy Maud Montgomery's *Anne of Green Gables,* it is Anne's spirited, free, affectionate personality that melts the stern Marilla into a loving and nurturing mentor. In each of these stories, and countless others, it is the child's behavior, once recognized and responded to with understanding and acceptance, that brings about beneficial change in the adult.

SEQUENCE (SURPRISES, REPLAYS, COLLABORATION)

Where signals and symbols need some decoding or interpreting, sequences come on a silver platter.

When child and parent engage in a dialogue or any series of interactions around one topic, they create a sequence together.

With some work, sequences can effect the self-awareness and growth of the parent as little else can. For instance, a child offers candid commentary on the parent's behavior. Now we can, as parents, initiate a sequence by making a comment or asking a question phrased in such a way as to invite our child's unselfconscious response. Sometimes sequences begin with a display of affection, an unsettling remark, or an embarrassing question from our child. If we are able to tolerate that discomfort for a moment and let what happened sink in, we can be rewarded with remarkably poignant, powerful insights. Our children's unique place in our lives can motivate us to a new awareness or a difficult change.

One of our country's past Secretary of Health, Education and Welfare, a heavy smoker, asked his thirteen-year-old son what he wanted most for his upcoming birthday. The boy looked at him with some hesitation, hugged him and said, "Dad, I wish you'd stop smoking. I'm worried about you and I don't want you to get sick."

This hard-working, stressed, public official was stunned. Smoking had been discussed before in the family. It was not the first time he had heard about it. What could he say? How could he deny his son's wish, so unselfishly put, and so in line with his official function?

Not only did the boy get his dearest wish, but the secretary, now an ex-smoker, became instrumental in the national smoking cessation campaign.

Sequences can be very far reaching! They come in so many varieties that it may be helpful to distinguish a few broad categories. Children provoke responses from us in different ways. They play different roles in each of these interactions. When we have our eyes and ears open, the end result is the same, and it is yet another step along the journey of our growth together.

SEQUENCE AS SURPRISE/INSIGHT

Looking at the world from its own perspective, sooner or later a child will do or say something startling to the parent. Kids can be quite intuitive to the undercurrents in the home or to our preoccupations. They can be unconventional in their candor. Their comments, stripped of artifice or inhibition, can go to the heart of the matter and touch a deep nerve. Less burdened by our adult repression and prejudices, they can see things with un-adult-erated vision. The tale of *The Emperor's New Clothes* is a funny illustration.

Hans Christian Andersen's tale has two swindlers arrive in town with the claim that they could weave such a refined cloth that it would be invisible to anyone who was not fit for his office or was impossibly dull. The emperor promptly ordered a suit to be made for him. Courtiers, inspecting the weaving, could not see anything, but said nothing for fear of being found to be unfit or dull. They ended up praising its refined qualities. When finally the emperor himself walked in procession with his "new clothes" on, the whole populace cheered and admired their beauty, none wanting to be found unfit or dull. Finally, a small child said, "But he has nothing on!" The rumor spread and all saw the emperor naked.

It wasn't for nothing that Andersen chose a child to reveal the naked truth. (We are not told what the effect on the emperor was).

Illuminations like these can be embarrassing, funny, or irritating in their straightforwardness. But who can quarrel with them, or with the child? By admitting their validity, they can become valuable clues to our self-understanding and catalysts for change. Out of the mouth of babes…

We have seen an example of this already in Tommy (p. 12), and in my children's comments about the "water out of the rock" and the "crooked roots." Here follows another:

Dan works long hours in a stressful, competitive business. Once he gets home, he thinks he's left the aggravation of the day at the office, but often he spends dinnertime criticizing his wife and barking at the kids. One day he overhears his son, six-year-old Steve, asking his mother: "How come Daddy yells so much when he comes home? Does he hate coming home that much?"

At first Dan felt insulted by Steve's question. Although his wife had protested his behavior before, he had always shrugged it off. "You're too sensitive," he told her. But the sadness and yearning in his son's voice got to him and he realized that Steve's comment was uncomfortably close to the truth. He did not hate coming home, per se, but because he was angry on the way home, he had carried his anger with him into the home and had dumped it on his family.

Where did it come from? He started to ask himself questions. He remembered his father's homecomings and they were not as bad as his. His dad was his own boss. He did not have to hold in his anger and resentment in the workplace.

Steve's complaint had set a process in motion that led Dan to the source of his anger and his poor way of dealing with it. He was ready now to find another way.

SEQUENCE AS REPLAY EFFECTS

Of all the child-effects we encounter in this book, replay effects is the category that has received the most attention in professional literature. It has to do with the remarkable ease with which we parents identify with our children; an ease that carries its own load of advantages and disadvantages.

A "replay" happens when our children meet the same trials and tribulations that we confronted when we grew up. This allows us an emotional replay. Just observing our kids or talking with them about these situations can inspire and motivate us to try one more time to tackle the old challenge, but now in a new way. "If you can do it, so can I!"

The "that's me" feeling, this immediate identification with our children, may be based on a unique parental bond: we were present at their creation. "This child is my blood and bones." It persists even after the young person has found his or her own place in the adult world.

The drawback of this strong identification is over-identification. When this happens, we no longer distinguish the child, its emotions, motives, etc., as separate from ourselves, especially when the child hasn't decided yet what it feels and looks to us for clues.

When we see our child hit a snag we have two choices: to make the child feel as we do ("I just *know* how angry, sad, happy, etc., you feel!"). Or we can allow the child to find its own emotional way and define its own reaction and become authentic. Only then can we compare what the child says with what we had expected, draw some conclusions, and learn from the difference. Without respect for the "otherness" of the child, we can't expect a real sequence.

We already say one example of a replay with Frank (p. 8), but here comes Louise's.

Louise put a lot of energy into making plans and organizing activities. As a child she had always dreaded feeling left out of anything. It was a form of rejection that she could not cope with. As a result, she could be unusually disappointed when plans fell flat, even as an adult. A rained-out picnic, a sold-out movie, distressed her. On a stormy day in March, she and her ten-year-old son, Jason, had tickets for the circus; a special treat they planned weeks ahead.

When they arrived, they were told the high winds had made use of the tent hazardous. The show was cancelled. Louise was beside herself. She tried to trade in her ticket, but found no good date. Now they might miss the show altogether! In the car going home, she complained a few times about the disappointment, apologizing each time to Jason.

Then she noticed that he did not seem to be as upset as she was. "Aren't you disappointed?" she asked him. "I thought you couldn't wait to see the circus."

"It's OK, Mom," he said. "I don't mind waiting a few more weeks."

"But what if we miss it entirely this year?" she wanted to know.

"Well," Jason said, "there's always next year!"

Louise was impressed by how mature Jason's reaction was. She was the one acting like a ten-year-old! He could evidently be a lot more accepting and flexible than she was in this kind of situation. She kept watching Jason and how he handled these disappointments and tried to recast her own. She would cheer herself on with, "There's always next year!"

SEQUENCE AS COLLABORATION

When we cultivate receptiveness to our children's contributions, *collaborations* with them can be the result. It is a unique adventure of growing up together. It is a deliberate process of mutual influence with low defensiveness—a true partnership in development. We accept from our children what we all too often reject from adults, even from close friends or one's spouse. A comment made in a neutral, kidding or loving tone from one of our children will often hit the mark. We are far more willing to listen to it and take it to heart. When collaboration takes place, parents and children truly help each other along the journey of life.

Collaboration is a process. It usually means a lifelong series of sequences. This is, without a doubt, the greatest gain of parenthood.

Ted was a devoted family man in his early forties. He and Sharon had a good marriage and three children. Between them was a wholesome, open and loving relationship. Ted's own background was less comfortable. His parents divorced after his thirteenth birthday, leaving him and his ten-year-old sister, Kate, in the care of their chronically depressed mother, who could barely cope. Ted had to grow up quickly. He became Kate's protector and scrutinized her activities and friends. Even after Kate married and had children of her own, Ted continued to act as if she were his daughter, coaching her when he got a chance.

Ted had dismissed his wife's statements that Kate and her husband might resent his intrusions into their lives. "Nobody understands how anxious I get when I worry about her," he told his wife. "It drives me nuts thinking they might not be doing well." Ted's wife eventually gave up trying to change his protective attitude towards his sister.

One Thanksgiving brought both families together. Ted began his usual fussing after Kate had left. Why didn't she get braces for her daughter's teeth? Did she not see her son was developing a weight problem? As he went on, he noticed that Sharon and the kids weren't really taking him seriously. He fell silent. Then Andrea, their daughter of seventeen, and independent young woman, stopped laughing and said calmly, "Dad, just let her go. You don't have to take care of Aunt Kate anymore. She is doing just fine."

His daughter's comment got through. Ted didn't want to admit it, but she was right. Kate was old enough to make her own decisions. He changed the subject.

Later, taking his problem to a deeper level, he asked Andrea if she wanted to know why he worried so much about Kate. "I know you had to take care of Aunt Kate when she was young. You must have been a great big brother! I know I wouldn't have wanted that kind of responsibility. Not at that age. Be glad that now you don't have to do it any more."

Andrea's empathy allowed Ted to admit that he sometimes had resented the role that was thrust upon him. Andrea had taken the problem yet one step further, showing him that his resentment was legitimate. He had felt guilty if he didn't worry about Kate. It was a vicious cycle. Andrea, speaking as the "the other daughter," had given him permission to let go. The earlier discussions with Sharon could never have reached this crucial point. His wife could not see him as someone who, ultimately, wanted to be free of the responsibility for his sister. But Andrea did. She could speak for Kate. Ted could finally begin to look at Kate as the adult she was.

Collaboration, as between Andrea and Ted, is the ultimate compliment parent and child can pay each other. When we engage our children in collaboration, they get to feel not only loved, but respected, included and trusted. There can be risks of over-identification, and they are discussed on p. 20.

Collaboration also promotes in children the realization that their contributions are truly valued and that they have some power to shape their fate. This is precisely how independent, autonomous people in relationships like to feel. Raising children becomes more enjoyable and effective in such a democratic family where power is gradually shared. It is a good start on our road to "life, liberty and the pursuit of happiness."

PARENTAL DEVELOPMENT
Depends on Receptivity to Child Effects

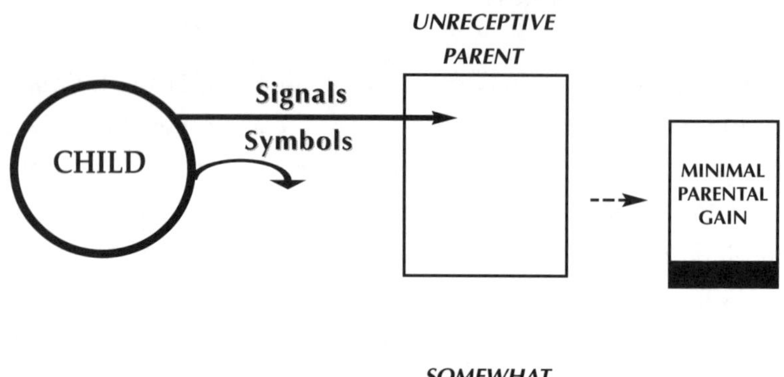

UNRECEPTIVE
PARENT
Signals
Symbols
CHILD
MINIMAL
PARENTAL
GAIN

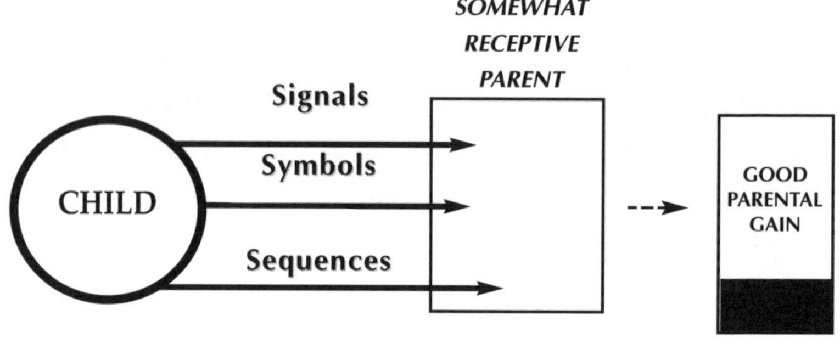

SOMEWHAT
RECEPTIVE
PARENT
Signals
Symbols
CHILD
Sequences
GOOD
PARENTAL
GAIN

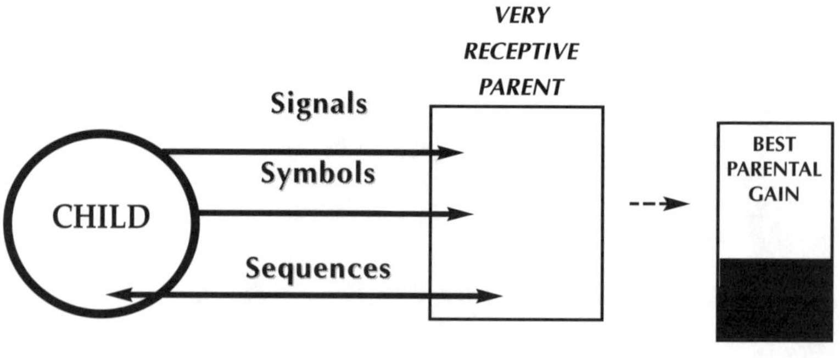

VERY
RECEPTIVE
PARENT
Signals
Symbols
CHILD
Sequences
BEST
PARENTAL
GAIN

CHAPTER TWO

Adult Development:
A Brief Review of the Idea and its History.
Where do I fit in? What is the role of my child?

In youth you find out what you care to do and care to be—even in changing roles. In young adulthood you learn whom you care to be with. In adulthood, however, you learn to know what and whom you can take care of. Erikson[iv]

When we survey the human life span from birth to death, we find it impossible to describe what we see unless we parcel it up in periods. These stages are often defined by their most salient characteristics.

The Greek legislator and poet, Solon (638-560 B.C.E.), and the Chinese sage, K'ung-Fu-Tzu (Master K'ung or Confucius, (551-479 B.C.E.), already had "road maps" for our life-journey. Perhaps the best known to Western readers is Shakespeare's:

All the world's a stage
and all the men and women merely players.
They have their exits and their entrances,
and one man in his time plays many parts,
his acts being seven ages. At first the <u>infant</u>
mewling and puking in the nurses' arms,

and then the whining <u>schoolboy</u>, with his satchel
and shining morning face, creeping like snail
unwillingly to school. And then the <u>lover</u>,
sighing like furnace, with a woeful ballad
made to his mistress' eyebrow. Then the <u>soldier</u>,
full of strange oaths and bearded like the pard,
jealous in honour, sudden and quick in quarrel,
seeking the bubble reputation
even in cannon's mouth. And then the <u>justice</u>,
in fair round belly with good capon lined,
with eyes severe and beard of formal cut,
full of wise saws and modern instances;
and so he plays his part. The <u>sixth age</u> shifts
into the lean and slippered pantaloon,
with spectacles on nose and pouch on side;
his youthful hose, well saved, a world too wide
for his shrunk shank; and his big manly voice,
turning again towards childish treble, pipes,
and whistles in his sound. <u>Last scene</u> of all,
that ends this strange eventful history,
is second childishness and mere oblivion,
sans teeth, sans eyes, sans taste, sans everything.[v]

For thousands of year, poets and philosophers of all great cultures have seen our life in steps or stages, as an onward movement through a necessary succession, each step with its own responsibilities and privileges, joys and sorrows.

It strikes us that, even in olden times, adulthood was seen as more than a tapering off towards the final exit. We move from the fertilized egg, to the explosive protoplasm, to the socialized, educated citizen who thinks, dances, sings, loves and prays. We are formed by influences beyond our control; the scenarios of nature and nurture. But as adults, as mostly formed individuals, we can still write variations on our limited themes: our character. Adults can be more active in determining the flow of this chapter of our lives. Here our children come into the picture. This is the theme of this book. Children have a privileged status in our lives. It gives them a hotline through which they exercise a powerful effect on us and our adult development, if only we let them.

When we talk about adult development from the nurture point of view, we are including both our inner, mental workings and our outer conduct: our behavior and relationships. How we feel about ourselves makes a difference in how we relate to others. How others treat us, what they show or teach us, can become a part of how we feel and behave. If these interactions are prolonged or intense, they can change our character.

The branch of psychology that studies human development has long been under the spell of the Freudian psychoanalytic interest in how children grow up. This is known as childhood development. The impetus for this interest came from the need to understand what makes adults tick. Using the regressive method (searching for prior causes of a current event), causes were assumed in, or even before, childhood. A trauma, conflict or empathetic failure in Grandma's early childhood could play itself out in her adult character, which in turn determined how she raised her son, who in his turn influenced her grandchild, which could be you. The child was father (mother) to the man (woman) under study. Could we go beyond the womb? Of course we could; we had to. The existing theories of child development were not comprehensive enough, they were too "vertical." We leave aside the nature aspect of development, (the theories of genetic programming), the complimentary side of the nurture aspect. We stick to the child-parent interaction.

Charles Darwin (1809-1882) introduced the idea of development. He proposed a continuous differentiation from simple to more complex forms and an integration of new elements into the next step of an ongoing evolution. This idea combined continuity with changes over time. Applying this idea, Erik Erikson (1902-1994), writing in the late fifties, carried Freud's ideas on childhood psychosexual development over into human psychological development. He divided the human life span into eight stages, the last three of which occur during adulthood. Daniel Levinson prefers to organize adult life into "seasons," each with its own specific set of topics and questions.

Researches may differ over stages and levels, but they do share the same fundamental premise: all through our adult lives we continue to change and evolve. Like our development in childhood, since some of what we experience is common to all of us, we can even anticipate some of the pressure for changes in our life, although it will be more difficult to predict the specifics of it. For example, we will probably lose at least one parent or get a grandchild at some time, but we cannot know beforehand how we shall react to those events.

When events in our lives require us to change in significant ways, we may feel confused or upset, even if we recognize the need to adapt. In many cases these changes stir up unfinished business from our childhood, when having to adapt was the order of the day. Through this process of periodic assessment and adjustment, we deepen and refine our sense of who we are. This is easy for some of us, but for others it can cause periods of intense turmoil. No wonder that many mythologies have metaphors for adult development such as a journey, a quest, or a series of ordeals to reach a goal of supreme value.

The Inner Journey

Serious thinking about adult development started with Carl Gustav Jung (1875-1961). Sigmund Freud (1856-1939) had less interest in how adults continue to grow. Of Freud's many contributions, two became incorporated into current theories of adult development. First, development proceeds in stages. Second, impulses, thoughts and feelings outside of our conscious awareness influence its progress.

By studying himself and his patients, primarily members of the Victorian Viennese middle class, Freud concluded that childhood, notably the first five years of life, was the critical time for all psychological growth. He saw our psychological development as a series of stages that started in infancy and ended in late adolescence. Ideally, our progress through these stages should lead us from infantile dependency to adult independence. Adulthood, which began for Freud with our psychological disengagement from our parents in adolescence, is characterized by mature sexuality, our ability to form committed love relationships and a consistent ability to work.

Jung, a Swiss psychoanalyst and one-time associate of Freud's, was the first to study psychological development during adulthood. Jung agreed with Freud's perception that psychological processes outside of our awareness could have an influence on us, but in Jung's view, neither sexuality nor past childhood experiences deserved the exclusive importance which Freud accorded them. Jung widened the scope and believed that our personalities are also shaped by current events and by our goals and aspirations for the future.

Jung's work helped establish the idea that we have important psychological work to accomplish as adults. Far from coming to a crawl after adolescence, our psychological growth can continue vigorously through the rest of our lives if we are up to the task.

Jung's interest was captured by outwardly successful patients who seemed to have lost their bearings in life. Most of these patients were middle-aged or older. The Freudian theory that sought the origin of their problems in unresolved childhood conflicts appeared insufficient to Jung. For him, the end point of life's heroic journey was the full realization of our inherent potential through the integration of the contrasting tendencies in our identity instead of manifesting only one aspect at the expense of its opposite (masculine - feminine, introvert-extrovert, etc.). Jung called this goal individuation.

Relying on one aspect of our personality and neglecting its opposite tendency can eventually lead us to a crisis. Jung was the first to draw attention to the turmoil which men and women in the middle period of their adult lives undergo: "a psychic revolution of life's noon."[iii]

Popularization of this early insight led to the misnomer "midlife crisis". However, not all developmentalists agree with this concept.[vi] This collapse of our previous view of ourselves and our world challenges us to reassess our lives and may allow the neglected aspects of our personality a greater freedom to assert themselves. A compliant, reserved woman may experiment with expressing herself; a workaholic father may, belatedly, discover a nurturing side of himself that wants to connect with his children.

We know that people, even twosomes, do not exist in a social or cultural vacuum. We need a bridge to our human world of fellow beings. This bridge has to be crossed to reach a fuller understanding of how we come to be who we are and can become what we are not. The time was ripe for Erikson.

FROM PRIVATE JOURNEY TO PUBLIC LIFE

The work of Erik Erikson began to offer a bridge between the theories about how our psyche is formed by our intimate interactions and the emerging theories that include the shaping factors of human culture and society.

Erikson, a child psychoanalyst, set out to examine the patterns of development in groups of people leading ordinary lives.

His research and personal experience in a variety of cultures convinced him that individuals in societies influence each other. Children are molded in part by the expectations and traditions of their societies; societies depend on, and are continuously renewed by, successive cohorts of grown-up children.

Erikson's focus on the formation of identity allowed him to study the give-and-take further shaping our character.

Who we are has both individual and collective origins. As individuals we have a sense of self that remains constant over time, that we carry from one stage of our development to the next. At the same time, we incorporate into our identity certain attitudes and ideals that we share with our social groups of our culture.

Erikson assigned eight stages to the human life span. In each stage we are faced with a developmental challenge in the form of a real-life task. These tasks are set by our evolving capabilities and the escalating demands of our social world. For example, in Erikson's first stage, the first year of infancy, the baby's task is to develop a basic sense of trust in self and the world, which is the cornerstone of a healthy personality. Since most of a baby's world is composed of the parents, success or failure in building trust will, to some degree, depend on the consistency of the parents' behavior. The baby gradually learns to rely on being taken care of, loved "imperfectly," and learns trust nevertheless and with it, to trust the world. A measure of frustration seems indispensable for building realistic trust.

The names of Eriksonian stages refer to the outcome of that stage's main task. For instance, basic trust versus mistrust, as in the above example. The last three stages occupy adulthood. They are: intimacy versus isolation, generativity versus stagnation, and integrity versus despair.

Mastering the task of one stage more or less successfully allows us to proceed to the next stage, which is built on the previous one. Trusting that someone cares, for instance, includes tolerating that this person cares for others as well, such as a spouse, siblings, etc. Our wishes need neither immediate nor complete satisfaction for trust and love to be maintained. From this solid base we can move on to the next phase, and proceed to explore the world at large.

In the _adult stages_, we generally enlarge our connections and concerns beyond ourselves, first to a loved one, then to children, then to an extended family that may include others as well, or to an even larger community through political or religious activities. From our family of origin we move to the family we establish as adults, and hence to the family of mankind, shedding receptive passivity for active participation, and moving from dependency to autonomy, inter-dependence and service.

Erikson's first _adult stage,_ "intimacy versus isolation," generally coincides with our twenties. During this time we relate to peers and friends through competition, sex, or cooperation. Our task during these years is learning how to form a mutually satisfying relationship with a sexual partner. Love is redefined again. The capacity for intimacy with another person lays the foundation for family life, which is our next stage.

The _second stage_ of adulthood concerns the task of caring for a younger generation. Meeting this task is called "generativity." Failure to include this aspect into our identity can lead to stagnation. Generativity is the willingness to act as a guide and mentor, not just for our own children, but for all those who will follow us.

Generativity may extend beyond the immediate context of family life and outlast the immediate years of childrearing. A senior member of a law firm who helps a young associate establish himself, or a retired person who devotes much of her free time to activities which will benefit the coming generation, are both engaging in generative activities. Self-absorption, expending our efforts mainly to benefit to ourselves, can lead to a sense that we're not producing anything of lasting value. The future recedes and stagnation sets in.

Since this book deals with the role of children in adult development, I will focus mostly on this middle part of adult life.

For Erikson's _last adult stage,_ "integrity versus despair," the task is to maintain the essence of what we have been and can still be while coming to terms with the reality that we will be no more. With integrity comes the sense that, on balance, we haven't wasted all of our opportunities, that our lives have meaning and significance. "Death destroys a man, but the idea of death saves him," said Forster.[vii] With integrity we face our own end without bitterness or a sense of having failed. We also may provide an inspiration for those coming after us who look for models in their own approaches to aging.

Integrity's dark shadow is despair. When the pieces of our lives do not and will not fit together, the puzzle remains, along with the frustrations of being old and the encroaching losses. Children and grandchildren can still play a role in our development even at this stage. Grandchildren often bring out aspects of their grandparents' personalities that are completely unfamiliar to the grandparents' own children. Marcel Proust[viii] found the following metaphor for this interesting phenomenon:

The character we exhibit in the latter half of our lives need not necessarily be, though it often is, our original character, developed further, dried up, exaggerated, or diminished. It can be its exact opposite, like a suit worn inside out.

In the early 1980s, Erikson revised his stages to accommodate a period of prolonged vigor in older people. He distinguished between elders, those described originally as: "the few wise men and women who quietly lived up to their stage-appropriate assignment and knew how to die with some dignity," and elderlies, those people who are active and whose lives seem to extend the generative period of middle adulthood.[ix]

Erikson's writings expanded and legitimized the field of adult development. Researcher George Vaillant has validated components of his thinking. In a study comparing the development of a group of college students and inner city young men, Vaillant found strong evidence of Erikson's developmental stages. He also found that social class and education had little bearing on the progress of adult development. Although Vaillant found a wide variation in the ages of the men during the beginning and end of any specific stage, he also found that all of the men mastered adult developmental tasks in the same sequence.[x] It thus seems that we may postpone or delay a stage, but we may not skip it.

TIMETABLES

Where do I fit in? What role does my child play?

Most of us have had a sense of our lives shifting to another gear. It may be a sudden conviction that our present goals and relationships are no longer satisfying, or we may notice that we've revised our view of the world and our place it in. A conviction that there is not much time left may have replaced a previous sense of unlimited potential. Some of these feelings are rooted in social reality. We tend to listen to society's expectations and move from a single life to settling down, marriage, children, and a responsible career (or various alternative variations of this theme). Other times it may derive from the contrast with our parents' lives: "My father made a success of his business by the time he was thirty, but I'm almost thirty-five and I'm still working for someone else." Still others are tied to our biology, such as childbearing or feeling the loss of physical prowess. We get a sense of a timetable and our place in it.

The many roads through maturity have spawned studies describing how we change after growing up. Levinson's *The Seasons of a Man's Life*[xi] is based on interviews with forty men from diverse backgrounds. Also published that year was Roger Gould's *Transformations,* using information he gleaned from interviews with hundreds of men and women.[xii] The work of both men remains valuable. Their conclusions are included in the developmental timetables beginning on page 39. This table partitions adult life into stages and lists important themes, developmental tasks and life events characteristic of each stage, as well as the role our children play along the way.

As we look at this timetable it yields some interesting insights. Levinson and Gould speak of a dream, beginning in our twenties, of what we hope to achieve in life. Its theme may be a career direction, such as "I want to be a great artist," or ideas about one's life, like "living with a husband and two kids in the country, yet with the time for a part time career." How much of the dream we realized or have to change gives us a yardstick for our developmental progress. At this period in life, our still young children will mostly exert their formative influence on us through symbols and signals.

Let us consider the role of such a dream. In our twenties we often have overblown aspirations. Bacon noticed it: "Young men are fitter to invent than to judge; fitter for execution than for counsel; and fitter for new projects than for settled business."[xiii] Peering into the mists of the future we like to see ourselves as great leaders, athletes, or successful professionals. The dream's glory can sustain us during the early years of establishing ourselves when work in our chosen fields may be tedious or very demanding. But as we grow older, we slowly, sometimes rudely, wake up and see what is left of the dream. This review often starts in our late thirties and early forties. It initiates the mid-life transition. The popular "mid-life crisis" is a misnomer. To continue our growth we need to reconcile dream with reality.

The wish to have kids sets the stage for this dream, easing the transition from a single life to a plural life. The care of children and their responses to us, reward us in those tough early years and keep us going. The choices they force upon us later lead to a review of our values (Do I really need to make more money? How important is time spent with them?). They help us re-define the dream within the limits of the possible and the practicable. As we will see later, even our conversations with them can get us unstuck when we find ourselves in a rut. This is the time of symbols and possibly sequences.

Much of the research on adult development has been done with men. Do men and women develop differently? Carol Gilligan studied moral development in women and men. She concluded that men tend to apply abstract principles of ethics to moral dilemma's, where as women are inclined to decide on the basis of the consequences of their decisions on others.[xiv] The differences in the timetable on page 39 need a grain of salt. Researchers consider that men and women develop according to their own timetables, although whether the differences are as widespread as these timetables suggest is still controversial. We obviously need more studies with both genders over longer periods of time to refine our understanding of what any real differences really mean.

This kind of research is difficult. Social and demographic conditions change rapidly. Decades have elapsed since Erikson, Gould, et al., have done their work. Sexual partners today frequently live together, with or without ultimately getting married. Couples who do marry are more likely to divorce. The age of entry into the workplace varies with the economic situation. Divorce, changing social mores and economic necessity have both lowered the age and increased the number of women entering the job market. These women are realizing their own dreams and following their own career paths, instead of simply looking for a job.

These changes have disrupted the neat scheduling of stages in our lives. Instead of facing certain developmental challenges only once in a lifetime, such as marrying, starting a family, or launching a career, we may now have to face them twice or three times. Developmental stages for women, especially for women with serious professional aspirations, may include some tasks which men don't face. These may include suspending career during the children's infancy, resuming a career, or for those who have postponed a decision about having children until their late thirties, facing a dilemma as the end of their childbearing years draws near.

More studies about adult development will probably follow. Can we already say what the little we know means for us now? From my own experience and from those I have talked with and have been able to observe over time, I do get the clear impression that few of us have followed the steps and stages of the adult developmental dance with the precision of a ballerina. It seems to be much more like a stop-and-go, muddle-through, hurry up, or slowly amble. Only in looking back may we discern a semblance of regularity. As it was developing, it never felt in any way schematic or predictable. This trail guide of the developmental stages is of limited value to us as long as we are on the road moving through the new, strange countryside where we meet sudden detours. These can be where a famine breaks out, new bridges are being built, rivers overflow, wells dry up, and oil fields are being discovered. To say nothing of unexpected company!

Timetables are therefore no blueprints. The one provided on page 39 needs constant revision. It cannot be more than only a rough sketch of a trail guide. Yet, a timetable can still help us to make sense out of some of the puzzling shifts in the course we have already experienced, while helping us to anticipate some of the challenges still to come. If we can anticipate, we can blunt some of the impact and prepare the ground for the inevitable change.

If at the same time we can allow our children a limited partnership in this venture of our unfolding lives, we shall be able to make the going a lot more interesting, rewarding and less troublesome. Their thoughts, words and actions help us understand how we became who we are, and help us become who we want to be.

DEVELOPMENTAL TIMETABLE

PULLING UP ROOTS (16-21)

*Leaving the Family - physical, psychological and social separation from parents
*Sexual and Personal Identity Consolidation

MALES	_BOTH_	_FEMALES_
	Start college or first job	
	Search for mate and career (plan)	

Search for mentor

Identity defined through self, spouse, peers, less through parents. Peers sustain separation

GETTING INTO THE ADULT WORLD (22-28)

*Life project constructed
*Commitments made - and seen as irrevocable
*Develop capacity for sustained intimacy

MALES	_BOTH_	_FEMALES_
Build the dream		Build the nest
	Complete education	
Launch career	Secure a mate	Secure a mentor
Support husband's dream		
Parental role definition		Bear children; Motherhood

(Child-effects mostly signals and symbols)

PUTTING DOWN ROOTS (29-36)

*Rooting and Branching Out

*First Signs of Aging

MALES	_BOTH_	_FEMALES_
Pursuit of dream, career		Family obligations vs.
Career		aspirations
Concern with physical		Search for balance
Fitness		

Childbearing responsibilities shared or not, and how
(child-effects: symbols and sequences)

MID-LIFE TRANSITION (37-43)

*Time shift: growing up to growing old
*Challenging passage
*Identity Review: sexual, personal, social

MALES	BOTH	FEMALES
Dream - reality gap		Building own dream
Occupational die is cast		Seek career and education
Compromises to be made	New sense of potential	

Marital instability
Empty nest syndrome
Enlarging bond with children based on reciprocity, equality
(child-effect: promoting sequences)

MID ADULTHOOD (44-50)

*Restabilization
* "Best Time of Life"
*Renew social activities
*Manage three-generation family relationships

MALES	BOTH	FEMALES
Dream reconciled		Dream developed
Mentor no longer needed		New life constructed
Serve as mentor to youth		Complete education
	Marital and social life balanced	
	Signs of aging	
	Beginning grandparenthood	

LATE ADULTHOOD (51-60)

*Review of life course
*Re-awakening spiritual life
*Generativity
*Adjustment, acceptance of aging

MALES	BOTH	FEMALES
Capping career		Pursuit of dream, career
	Creating social heirs	
	Sponsoring the young	
Emergence of nurturing aspect		Familiarity with power

(Child-effects in grandparenthood, the "third chance")

OLD AGE (61 AND OVER)

*Life review
*Preparation for retirement
*Search for security, financial support
*Renewed spiritual quest
*Aging more pronounced
*Integrity vs. despair

MALES	BOTH	FEMALES
Retirement		Capping a career
Develop leisure interests		Rehearsal for widowhood
(often complimentary to career)		
	Renew friendships, family ties	
	New communities of living	

(child-effects: from two generations, all categories)

CHAPTER THREE

BECOMING A PARENT:
PREGNANCY AND BABY

"...If I hadn't had a child, I'd never have know that most elemental, direct, true relationship. I don't know if I'd fully understand the values of society that I prize. I would have missed the mystery of life and death. Not to know how a child grows, the wonder of a newborn's hand...I have been fortunate".
Dianne Feinstein, Mayor of San Francisco

Ask any parent you know and they will tell you that having a baby changed their lives and changed them as people as well. Children have a formative influence on their parents, even before they are born! This starts when we decide to become a parent, anticipate parenthood, and live through the pregnancy and birth. These are times of both joy and fear, deep reflection and sudden anxieties. We are wondering and made aware of life, ourselves and our course in life as nothing ever before.

For women, pregnancy, labor and delivery are physical and emotional storms. For men, the changes are less turbulent, but equally profound. This early phase of parenthood evokes memories of our childhood and our own parents we are now beginning to identify with.[XV] The unborn starts the process of a new understanding of ourselves and our relations to others. The child yet to come already sets us firmly on our developmental journey as parents.

During this time we grapple with many of the major changes parenthood brings, such as a new identity and a new responsibility. This recasts our interactions with spouse, friends and relatives. We focus on major decisions, such as where to live and how to merge parenthood with our career.

As far as child-effects go, they are limited to signals. The moments of developmental progress of the baby reverberate in the lives of the prospective and new parents. But these signals sound loud and clear: the positive pregnancy test, the first visit to the obstetrician, hearing the fetal heartbeat, the first maternity clothes, and so on. Each one usually invokes complex emotions and is vividly remembered. They all carry the signal: "You are going to change drastically!"

Sharon, a thirty-two-year-old attorney, recalls exactly where she was when the doctor confirmed the diagnosis: "I was sitting on the edge of the bed, feeling slightly nauseous. It was 8:30 A.M. I had to wait to get through to my doctor's call-in time. George, my husband, was sitting next to me, ready to go to work, waiting impatiently. Finally I heard the doctor's voice and he said simply: 'Yes, you are pregnant. Congratulations!' I squeaked: 'Really?'. He went on to give me more details, but I barely heard him. George knew from my expression what it was. After I hung up we just stared at each other. He was stunned, too. We had made a baby!"

But the baby had made two parents! From that moment on its life, issuing from them, would continue to transform and influence them in major ways. We are so conditioned to look at this generational interchange from our own, our parental vantage point of parents influencing children, that we now need to re-focus on the neglected side, the countercurrent, and the child-effects on the parent.

Wasn't the birth of your child the biggest "first" of your life? The initial contact between mother, father and baby is a truly transformative family moment. We often retell our labor and delivery stories endlessly, having to integrate this transcending experience into our lives. We will remember this birth with the original rush of joy, worry and relief. Some postpartum mothers hear the story of their own birth from their mothers for the first time and are amazed at how much is remembered and cherished. For some women this is a time for a new kind of closeness with their mothers; they feel a cathartic sense of having lived and shared their mother's pain and pleasure. A new mother may also feel serene confirmation of now being a woman and a mother herself. It is the child who makes the parent come to life.

The early months of caring for an infant produce scores of signals and a few symbols. Amidst the mundane tasks of daily care are countless opportunities for us to become aware of and to examine our feelings. From the first bath, to the first smile, to the first outing, we are caught in a dizzying stream of getting to know our baby as well as ourselves. As parents, we can spot symbols among our reactions to the new responsibilities of child-care, or in our fears, frustrations and doubts (Why do I find this crying so disturbing? Where is this anger coming from, anyway?). We find them also in our triumphs and joys. A young father writes:" My purpose is to serve my children, not to excel elsewhere. In other words; having children makes it easier to disregard my imperfections. I'm just a parent."

Our parenthood compels us to re-evaluate our own parents as we remember them from our childhood. At the same time, we can, for the first time, identify with them as parents. What they did then and what we do now, allows for a re-experience and a review which can lead to a re-examination of problems that have not been resolved, this time with ourselves in the parental role. If we are willing to engage this process of associative remembering and reliving, we can give these problems a second look. Our child triggers this benefit of hindsight. We seem to get a second chance to come to terms with what eluded us before, when we were small and had so little power. We shall see many examples of parents availing themselves of this chance through all the growth-stages of the child, and how doing this nudges them along on their adult development.

MAKING THE DECISION

The "beginning parent" is usually between twenty and forty, in what Levinson called "early adulthood." (Although many unmarried teenagers and single adults become parents, I will discuss biological parenthood that occurs with a spouse or life-partner present. I shall deal with teenage parents and adoptive parents later on.)

Earlier developmental theories, such as Erikson's, were based on demographic patterns of marriage and parenthood in the 1940s and 1950s. Erikson assumed first-time parents to be between twenty and thirty. Today, first-time parents can be in their thirties or even older. Thus some younger couples are still struggling with the task of intimacy when they become parents, while the older ones are well underway to explore Erikson's notion of generativity.

When to have a child has become less predictable as many people marry later in life and have to balance career and education with their life decisions. The days of a single breadwinner who marries and establishes a family after his education has prepared him for life are over for many young people.

The early twenties are often a time of exploration, experimentation and growing up. This is what Levinson has called the "provisional years." Young people assume and then discard different identities before finding one that fits. They relish the freedom to pursue an unrealistic dream (pro athlete, Broadway star), a sweeping love affair, work at a variety of jobs, or dedicate their life to a single career. Gould observed that the twenties can also be a time of confidence and optimism. A twenty-two-year-old has the physical stamina and the emotional enthusiasm to advance a career by endless hours of overtime or additional training. The main task for this period is the establishment of intimacy (Erikson), finding and making friends, and more importantly, forming a mutually satisfying love relationship. For many young people, the conflicting developmental tasks of intimacy and identity make becoming a parent just too much; for others inevitable. For yet others, parenthood is acceptable, but not relevant. For these, a surprise event can trigger the decision process.

Barbara, a twenty-seven-year-old social worker, lived in a big house with several roommates. For her and her twenty-nine-year-old boyfriend, Logan, getting married and having children seemed a distant reality. Some day, yes, but not now. A graduate school friend had moved to a house in the country and just had a baby. She and her husband invited Barbara and Logan for a visit. When they arrived, they chanced upon a scene of domestic bliss: the friend nursing her infant in front of a wood-burning stove; the husband, in flannel shirt and blue jeans, boiling water for tea. Although the couple talked about the birth as traumatic—a rushed drive to the hospital two hours away, an emergency Caesarean—their life was serene and idyllic. Barbara had never seen a nursing mother before and was stunned by the young mother's radiance. She began to feel that she could be a mother like her friend. On the way home, she and Logan talked seriously about getting married, which they did soon after. Here we see how a child-effect can be extended to a friend of the parent! It enabled Barbara to envision herself in the role of mother.

Parents in their Twenties

The decision to have a baby, or an unexpected pregnancy, can result in a clash between the young parent's developmental task (intimacy), and the unceasing demands of a child. Erikson described this period as a "psychosocial moratorium; a socially sanctioned postponement of adult commitments in young lives fraught with identity confusion." Yet, for some couples, parenthood is a natural ideal and goes automatically with marriage. They expect it and are ready for it.

Phil, a twenty-six-year-old mechanic, knew that proposing marriage to Vicky meant starting a family right away. They both came from largely dysfunctional families and were looking forward to their own "dynasty" which, of course, would have to undo much of their own past pain. They lived together for a while enjoying the freedom of going out after work and trips on weekends, before they decided to get married. Becoming parents had been a part of their self-concept all along, and career considerations were secondary. They became each other's parent and soon had their own children and a good family life. (We first met Phil and Vicky in Chapter One).

For parents in their thirties, making the decision to have children is often a deliberate process, based on reaching a balance in their lives between postponements and deadlines. These couples wait until the time is right. Like Sharon and George, they've finished school, spent time on their careers, and decided on where and how they'd like to live. It remains a precarious balance. At a meeting of the three childcare experts Drs. Benjamin Spock, T. Berry Brazelton and Penelope Leach, in Cambridge, Mass. in 1988, they gave as their opinion that to balance work and family, parents must reorder their priorities and put their children before their jobs and possessions.[xvi]

Older first-time parents usually have come to terms with questions, such as independence from their own parents, competence , career choices, and stable relations with a mate and a circle of friends. All this does not mean that the effects of their children on their further growth will be any less profound, but the decision to have a child may propel the older future parent into an entirely new direction. The sense of responsibility may weigh heavier on them, more aware as they are of its consequences. They hesitate. They may need to recapture some of youth's playfulness and light touch. Lo and behold! Who would be better able than a child to prompt them in this direction?

Having a second or third child can have an equally significant impact on parental development. The first, the parent-maker, alters the marital dyad forever, playing on old rivalries of triangles and alliances. The second child confirms the parental identity and the family as a unit, but can strain its emotional and physical resources. Having more than one child may correspond more closely to the image that some people have about parenthood and family. They hope that it confirms them as competent parents. It seems to say: "We tried it, and we like it!"

One of these parents said: "I don't like the tidiness of one child, nor the symmetry of one child for each parent. I think we need a little more unpredictability, so we have to improvise all the time. I'd rather have a bunch of happy wildflowers in a jug than a single orchid in a vase." She had one more after her first baby and then a set of twins. They brought out the best in her as a mother.

No matter how ready most of us parents feel, we are totally unprepared for what comes at birth in two essential aspects: the child is irrevocable and non-elective. We cannot undo it and we did not choose it either. Unlike toys and other items, we can never return a child to the store. It is ours forever—though it is never completely ours. Right from the start it has a gender, a personality, and a mind all its own. Unlike anything else in life that we may have wished for and get, it is never quite what we wanted, nor will it turn out to be so. We do not find these two aspects in any other human relationship. This "no return" and "no choice" limits our expectations and opens doors to new possibilities we find with no one else. Child-effects are among those new possibilities.

PREGNANCY

The baby gives us nine months to prepare ourselves for its coming and for our new identity and image[xvii]. When the pregnancy is verified, most women are aware of a set of intense emotions, which range from joy and relief, to worry and panic.

Sharon vividly remembered hearing the news from her doctor and reacting with awe. She floated the rest of the day and thought of little else. Although she and her husband Kevin had been trying to conceive for six months, Sharon had little confidence that she could do so. At twenty-nine, she often felt intimidated by authority figures, and she remained highly dependent upon her mother and sister for companionship and support. Knowing that she had conceived made Sharon feel she was promoted. But her triumph was tempered by nausea. She became mildly depressed. After discussing her feelings with Kevin, she saw them as part of her self-doubts.

Trivial matters such as buying a coat, or weighty decisions

like choosing a job, used to make her nervous and unsure of herself. Despite her marriage and career, Sharon could hardly believe that she was a competent, independent adult. Could she really be carrying a normal life inside her? Would she be a good mother? But this time, she heeded the baby's signal. She could not doubt the reality of her conception.

Kevin had helped her see her doubts of motherhood as part of a pattern, but the baby had fulfilled a life's dream and dispelled a serious doubt she had about herself as a woman. This child, as yet unborn, allowed her to acquire a true sense of competence and let her feel, once and for all, grown-up.

A child of our own compels us to re-evaluate our relationship with our parents. During the pregnancy many of us have talked at length about our childhood, sometimes with our parents and often with others. We discuss their strengths and weaknesses, and what kind of parents they were. This often leads to a shift in the relationship with our parents, beginning in pregnancy and continuing throughout the early years of parenthood. Besides conflict and hurt, this reflection can bring reconciliation and healing.

Patty and Rick were a young couple expecting their first child. Rick had often envied Patty's relationship with her parents. His own parents, non-practicing Jews, had opposed his marrying Patty, who was from a Catholic background. Rick's parents' opposition was not so much to assimilation as it was to his moving away. It was a latent battle about his independence. Rick, like others in this dilemma, had recourse to an unacceptable action, which would force a separation that had not grown organically. It was a rupture and not an easing apart between parent and grown child. He married Patty. Rick's parents had refused to meet their daughter-in-law, so Rick declined to visit home without her. It was a standoff. As teachers, they would have a few weeks vacation around Christmas. Arguments around how to spend this time began to strain the marriage. Patty wanted to visit her parents; Rick wanted to go to the Caribbean: "We will never again have such a carefree time." Patty and Rick compromised on their vacation: three days with Patty's folks, followed by a week in Curaçao. Several months later their daughter was born. Rick mailed the first pictures home, telling how thrilled Patty's parents had been. Soon things started to change. Face-saving letters and phone calls preceded a visit. Rick's parents overcame their reluctance and crooned over their first grandchild. What an adorable baby!

Here the child, its coming and birth, had enabled a healing reconciliation through the effects of signals to Rick and his parents: "You are now promoted to parent and grandparent status! Your relation to each other is irrevocably changed." They could step over their reservations and claim their new status with pride and joy.

Parents who are about to become grandparents may react with joy, discomfort, or a mixture of both. They too, will notice a new set of child-effects. They may be uncomfortable accepting their son or daughter as a parent-to-be, finding such sexual maturity awkward, or rejoice in the continuation of the family line, trying to re-assert their parenthood and authority by giving endless advice.

Young women, still establishing their identities, may find pregnancy a way to separate themselves from their parents while identifying with them and reconciling the difficulties they may have had with them.[xviii] The child can lead us to feeling closer and more appreciative of our parents and encourage us to become aware of how we are different from them.

In short, what upheavals do we see in the wake of this blessed event! What loosening of ties, what rearranging of the inner furniture of our lives and personalities? If we realize the seismic changes brought about by the anticipation of a child, what tectonic shifts can we expect in our family once the new member is there to exert its influence, certainly on those willing to be affected by it? To get a glimpse of what can go on later in a family life, we read what a parent writes:

"It has been very revealing to me to visit my parents with my children. By seeing the way they react to their grandchildren, I have learned some interesting things about how I was (I believe) treated as a child. One day my son brought in his ball, caked with mud, and dropped it on the carpet. Grandmother came quickly, was upset and said, "Bad boy! Bad boy!" and took away the ball. Jeff seemed surprised but not upset. I was alarmed. How can anyone say that to a child? Yet it sounded familiar, coming from a previous world as it did, giving me a pang of sadness and latent frustration and self-doubt which I had not yet fully erased, and coming from such an incident. I stepped in, telling Jeff he had made a beautiful mess and saying to Grandma that Judy and I didn't like to say "bad boy," but prefer to give instructions. It is my fervent goal to correct in my children's lives the things that hurt me most in mine. I will also limit my children's exposure to their grandmother."

PREGNANCY AND CHANGE

During pregnancy we begin to ask ourselves seriously, what kind of parent do we want to become? We remember a few things we want to change. We have seen others and admired them. We want to emulate them. We have some ideas of our own. The nitty-gritty of working this out in practice comes from our responses to the real presence of the child.

Our response to the signal of the coming baby may range from a happy smile, to a mild musing, to a depression. Be that as

it may, each presents an opportunity for us to begin to understand a little bit more of ourselves, and the part of us yet unex-
plored: the parent part. How come I feel so different? What
makes me do things I never did before?

Stan, a successful businessman of thirty-nine, was used to
making decisions, being in charge, and having his orders obeyed.
Stan was also caring, generous and funny. When his wife of eight
years, Betsy, found out she was pregnant, Stan was mighty proud
and exhilarated about a new future project. He wanted to partic-
ipate in the pregnancy. He immersed himself in books about
pregnancy, childbirth, began to tell Betsy what she should eat
and what to avoid, which exercises to do, and what movies not
to see, all out of concern for the baby, of course. Fatherhood
brought out Stan's managerial skills, but Betsy did not seem to
need them. She became increasingly annoyed, telling him that
her pregnancy seemed to be his project, and that she resented it.
Stan was stunned. However, Betsy drew the line and forced him
to re-examine not only his behavior towards his pregnant wife,
but even how he acted towards others. Stan faced up to this task.

The baby thus had an important impact on Stan even before
it was born. He reined in his urge to take charge when it was not
needed nor welcomed—what a great asset for a father who wants
to help raise his kids!

The feeling of responsibility that parenthood brings is different from any other, due to the irrevocable nature of that relationship. Men who have been floundering or feeling stuck in their
jobs, may get a renewed sense of optimism and self-worth. They
may get determined to advance their careers. On the other hand,
men who are usually practical and prudent may start to buy lux-
ury items and go on expensive vacations to exploit their threatened freedom to its fullest. When marriage and parenthood are

perceived as burdens rather than opportunities, men and women can sometimes act rebelliously and less responsibly. From *A Streetcar named Desire* to *Gregory Girl* and *Heartburn*, literature and movies give us examples of men acting on their mixed feelings by having an affair while their wives are pregnant or in labor.

Women, as part of prenatal care, may significantly alter their habits regarding work, eating, drinking and recreation. For some women this may be the first time they have really changed some unhealthy habits. This can contribute to a new sense of importance, and a purposeful bolstering of their self-image. For many women pregnancy becomes a major boost in their capacity to develop feelings of altruism and self-sacrifice, both of which are needed ingredients of good mothering.

Altruism (the care for others) is scarce today. "Self" and "me" are in focus. Social critics point out that acquisitiveness and the rush to riches frays the social fabric. The vital glue of a society, the cement of a community, is mutuality and concern for others.

For some expectant mothers, the physical changes of pregnancy are frightening and ugly, even when most are temporary. The expanding space for the coming baby gives rise to anxieties and resentments as well as conflicts. The thought that nature, as in the rest of life, makes a trade-off, or that babies rarely come without leaving their traces on their mothers' bodies, is not a source of pride and comfort for these young mothers.

The child in the womb is itself a signal of portentous changes yet to come. It confronts us with merciful gradualness and patience with the adjustments we need to make in our lives to meet this new challenge, and provides us unequalled opportunity for our growth as well. There are opportunities to explore new ways of doing old things, to try out neglected aspects of ourselves, and to discover new capabilities. The coming birth alters the personal landscape in ways we cannot foresee, much as the clouds, the shifting light and the seasons transform the familiar landscape.

The changes wrought by the birth of our child are truly miraculous. No other event has the same transformative power over us. We already looked at a few child-effects. For the purposes of this chapter, I shall limit myself to highlighting only three aspects of birth that offer developmental opportunities for parents.

The first one is that of *parent power*. For many of us, the birth of a child is the first experience we have as adults of making serious decisions that have a lasting effect on another person. Previous choices, such as what college to go to, or getting married, are usually made with help from parents or friends. But the naming of the baby, circumcision and how to respond to the child, make us responsible people with authority over another. Where family tradition or communal support are lacking, we turn to books about the process of giving birth and raising the child.[xix]

Today, many of us approach labor and delivery after months of intense preparation. The current doctrine prefers no drugs, no episiotomy, and home delivery, or at least a "birthing room" in the hospital. Even after such a natural birth, parents can feel shock and disappointment mingled with excitement and relief. Or, as a distraught father exclaimed: "Yes, of course I'm glad its body is all in one piece, but when she cries she really looks like, well, your mother." It is our moment of truth; we find out then and there that birth was only the starting signal of a prolonged period of tantalizing unpredictability and difficult choices. This very unpredictability makes labor and delivery one of the best introductions to parenthood. Besides an early confrontation with parental power, it also begins the process of learning to live with the limitations of that same power over the child. We cannot, we do not, and we should not even try to make the child what we want it to be, but only help it along in becoming what it might be.

We start to learn to sort out our fantasies from the realities of coming to terms with surprises, disappointments, and interruptions, so that we may move on to flexibility and acceptance.

Ben remembers the birth of his first child as a moment of triumph, despite the hassles and arguments surrounding the event. Even though he and his wife, Carla, had gone to childbirth classes and were shown the birthing room, he was unprepared for how angry he would feel about the interference of the hospital policies, the doctors, and the nurses. Carla's labor was protracted, the baby showed some fetal distress. The obstetrician made an emergency decision to do a Caesarean. Disappointed and frightened, Ben could only let them proceed. He was barred from the operating room. The baby was kept in a special nursery for observation for two days. Only after she was brought into the regular nursery and pronounced healthy and whole, did Ben loose it. He yelled at the nurses for not preparing Carla better; he interrogated the doctors about the Caesarean, he even blamed Carla for not trying harder to push. The next day he had calmed down. He apologized. He was grateful that the child was alright. But he remained resentful about how things had gone and vowed to use a different hospital next time.

Ben could have used his angry reaction to the baby's first appearance to his own advantage if he had explored the feelings that led up to his explosion. Feeling unexpectedly without control over the whole process had made him feel vulnerable, and unable to protect Carla. Watching her in pain made him feel helpless to an unbearable degree. Nothing went as was planned. He dealt with his frustrations by attacking others, as if it were better to make a victim than to be one, or shift the blame before it would land on him. He had felt assertive and strong again while angry, but like a heel after he calmed down.

This need for power and control, which ordinarily accompanies responsibility, can have disastrous effects on the child-parent relationship. Power-problems effectively sabotage the chances for the emergence of the most helpful child-effects, as we shall see later on. This can lead, in turn, to a stifled adult development, not to speak of the wounding of the child. Power and responsibility need to be balanced and shared between the spouses, and progressively shared with the growing child as well. A child's birth can begin to teach us this lesson quite forcefully, if we are ready to learn. Ben had a hard time with it, but perhaps we can learn from him.

The couple redefined is the second aspect of birth we want to look at. Ben's helpless rage with seeing Carla in pain is a natural reaction. Men report these feelings frequently when they recount stories of deliveries. It evokes images of what might go wrong, of mortality even so close to birth, and it hits home. This shock to the new parents can result in a new commitment to each other and the marriage, now illuminated by a sudden sense of preciousness. It can also be a startling moment of revelation, putting all of life in a new perspective. Sadly, it can go the other way as well, when the birth forces to the surface a hidden flaw in the parental bond.

George and Dianne had postponed their first baby. George liked their living-together years. He was attracted to Dianne and she doted on him. They had found each other soon after college and grew closer when George's parents broke up their stressful marriage. Dianne's mother had died when she was nine. She was raised by her older sister who married when she was sixteen. Now Dianne had convinced George that they would get married as soon as she got pregnant. George seemed to have settled in the prospect of imminent fatherhood and Dianne made room in her work schedule for the baby to come. Not long after they came home with the child, their difficulties began. George started to come home late from work. Dianne wanted him to take care of the night feedings. They could not agree on how to spend the weekends. Dianne wanted to rest or go out. George insisted on joining his fishing buddies he hadn't seen for a long time. When Dianne asked him why he was withdrawing, he said, "You spend all your time with him anyway!" "Him" was their son.

Things went from bad to worse as the baby got colicky. The pediatrician spotted the tension in Dianne, and took the time for a good history. "I can't help but hear three people crying!" she suggested sympathetically.

For the next visit she invited George to come in as well. Gently she asked if they each felt like crying sometimes, each one for nurturance, food, time, affection, but none feeling they were getting their fair share. "It all looked so good at first, but now all we do is argue," said Dianne.

"I didn't want to copy my parents' problems," said George. They were seen a few more times and then, with some coaching and support from the office nurse (herself an accomplished mother), they found a new balance between needing and giving care.

Here, the birth exposed a flaw in a marriage. Each expected the other to give the care they both wanted, but had not received, from their parents. The baby upset the scales with his crying needs and became the intruder, the competitor in what had been a workable, but chancy, arrangement. Out of frustration, each had responded by withdrawing into the role of a needy child— not a very sustainable position to be in as a parent!

Many men report that the birth experience made them take stock of their careers and other aspects of life. Suddenly the future does not seem endless any more. Things that didn't matter much before, now do, such as job-security and reasonable hours. Things that used to matter a lot like ambition or acquisitions, may matter less or in a different way. An increasing number of men cut back their work to spend more time with their families. Or they may increase their energy to "get ahead" to provide greater security or educational opportunities for their child.

Even when the reaction to labor and delivery is comical, it can be revealing.

David and Karen, a couple who knew they wanted only one child, couldn't agree on a name for the baby. Even in the idyllic first few days after birth, they bickered about it. Neither would compromise and the hospital required them to put something down on the form. Weeks later they realized their resistance to compromising had to do with their decision to have only one child and with the difficulty they had with sharing power. This was to be the first time, but certainly not the last. Once they understood that they had to learn fast, they laughed and agreed on a selection.

All this reflects our coming to terms with this bright nova in our firmament, this new star we now have to calculate our course by, this relationship that will not be broken, and with a person most dear whose personality we did not choose.

Realizing this, we now take a brief look at the third aspect of birth to focus on: *fantasy vs reality* (other aspects we have to skip for brevity's sake).

The birth fantasy is often followed by a baby fantasy. Gender, personality, size, and looks are all part of our idealized image of the baby and of parenthood. In the first few days, we grapple with the degree of mismatch between our expectations and reality. Even the way a newborn looks can surprise us. Most of them don't look like the prettified ads: plump, rosy and smiling. Parents often are dismayed to find their baby is blotchy, scrawny, too bald or too hairy, or with an odd-shaped head. Many parents, despite friends' stories, hope to come home with a baby who sleeps through the night, nurses every two hours on schedule, and never requires more than two changes of clothes a day. Parents who expect a baby who makes plenty of eye contact and is engaging, may feel bewildered by a passive, drowsy child who is quiet. The exhaustion of the early weeks and the lingering disappointment over a baby who is not the embodiment of our wishes and expectations, presents a new and yet profoundly liberating challenge to us. Why liberating? Well, not only is our child not the product of our wishes and fantasies, it never will be, nor can we try with impunity to mold it that way. It is who it is as it comes into our trust for a period of our shared life, to be nurtured, loved, protected and prepared for a life of its own.

Jerome Kagan, professor of developmental psychology at Harvard, said, " Most cultures don't believe that parents should assume the primary responsibility for the outcome of their children... It's not clear why we believe that what the parents do, primarily the mother, essentially controls all the child's development"[XX] Even psychotic mothers have been know to raise behaviorally relatively unharmed children. We do not have to do all of it, or blame ourselves for all of the outcome.

Perhaps one of the greatest fantasies and wishes about having a baby involves its "right" gender.

When Marilyn,28, the mother of a four-year-old girl, got the news that her baby was going to be a boy, she was upset and disappointed. "I have grown up with an older sister and I wanted to recreate that family for my daughter. Neither she nor I would know what to do with a baby brother. I had a sister, my mother had three. What did I know about raising boys? They are, except for my husband, of course, an alien species. But when I called an old friend of mine with the news and how it had upset me, she couldn't believe it.

"Are you kidding?" she said. "Don't you remember how much you always wanted to have a boy? In fourth grade you said you were eating lemons because your grandmother had told you that eating lemons insured a boy baby. I bet you're going to love him!"

When Marilyn hung up the phone she was surprised that she had not remembered that childhood incident. "I had totally forgotten it, perhaps because I was so caught up in being the mother of a daughter."

Here it is, that non-elective aspect of the child, its gender, which gave this mother a powerful signal. "I am what I am. I did not choose you either. We will now learn to live with and love each other in that light." This mother needed to widen her scope beyond her family of origin and her current family. She also had to connect again with her childhood wish and recapture a taste for newness of her life before she could do the same with her child. How would she have done that without this unsettling challenge of the signal? Doesn't Marilyn speak for all of us when she says, "What I got is not what I had prayed for, but what I needed more."

The Early Days

The signals from the newborn leave us parents with the sense that we are being acted upon, rather than being the ones in charge. Sometimes these signals evoke emotions that seem oddly out of place around a newborn's crib, such as sadness, apprehension, frustration, etc. But, like the evil fairies in the fairytales who come uninvited to the birthday party, they have to be rendered powerless, lest harm come to the child. This exorcism involves an unmasking of the true nature of the witch. So it is with these surprising feelings that don't seem to fit. The reward for our effort of examining this initial upset is an increased self-understanding and competence as a parent.

The invited guest at the party, the positive feelings of pleasure with the child, rarely are signals that raise problems, needing a reflection on our part. We smile when our baby smiles; we melt when she coos. But if we can learn to trace the unwelcome feelings that surface, we will transform a bewildering and overwhelming period into an illuminating time of self-awareness and personal growth. The baby who presents us with the puzzling return to an old psychological quandary, or an unexplained sense of insecurity or failure also invites us to resolve a problem we had turned our backs to. Dealing with signals in this way begins to lay the groundwork for creating successful sequences as you and your child grow older.

Daniel, a young architect, thought that everything was fine with his wife, Jocelyn, and their ten-day-old son, Andrew. The boy was an eager eater, spending most of his waking hours nursing. Jocelyn was breastfeeding effortlessly. One evening, as she was nursing Andy, she turned to Daniel and said, "You know, I feel a little mixed up while I'm nursing Andy, even sad sometimes. At the same time, I feel so close to him and warm. Isn't that strange?"

Daniel listened sympathetically. Later he commented, " She described feeling as though she had lost something, but we couldn't see quite what that had to do with anything. After all, we had just gained something." Daniel had suggested to Jocelyn that maybe her feelings might have to do with them being more vulnerable now, as new parents, and unsure of themselves. With all the phone calls and family visits, they had lost the easy life they had led up to then. Next, Daniel recalled that he too, on occasion had felt a pang of melancholy when he had picked up Andy in the middle of the night. Not as clearly as Jocelyn, but he had felt a little ill at ease and a little lonely, "I felt like a little kid, crying in bed and calling for my Mom and Dad to come and get me. I realized how ironic that was, because now I was the dad!". He shared this recollection with Jocelyn, and it sparked vivid memories in her of her mother rocking her out of a nightmare and soothing her with a song and some ginger ale when she was sick. The snuggly comfort of her mother's warm, flannel nightgown came back in a rush. "Her lap was the most comforting place in the world," Jocelyn said, smiling through her tears. Sitting quietly for a few moments, they let their realization sink in. "Now I'm the warm body in the flannel nightgown," Jocelyn said wistfully.

The obligations of parenting had become a reality for this couple. Paying attention to the reactions they experienced to their baby's early needs, they were able to listen to its signal-value. Now it was their turn to be a nurturing parent. But Jocelyn and Daniel first had to register their unexpected emotions, trace them, and connect with the sense of loss, before they could put their own childhood needs in this new perspective, and, as it were, transcend them. By identifying with Andrew, Daniel and Jocelyn could recapture some of the lost sweetness of being comforted. By identifying with their original caregiver, they added the new dimension of care giving to themselves. By listening to each other and pondering their feelings, their melancholy was supplanted by a novel sense of competence and satisfaction, with a note of wistful nostalgia for their own childhood.

Dealing with this incident in such a way established an important precedent for both Jocelyn and Daniel, and for their interactions with Andy. It confirmed their son as a potential ally in their own growth. By being receptive to the signal, soliciting help and mulling things over, Jocelyn had given her transition to motherhood a developmental boost. She had affirmed her closeness with her husband and forged an alliance with her son.

Having a second or third child causes a significant shift that can help move our developmental process along. These siblings cause a whole series of dynamic shifts in the family, and each of them offers new and different chances for adult development. We can't begin to explore all these ramifications in this book, however. I give only one example in which it took three babies for the mother to make a necessary step.

Concepta was twenty-four and unmarried. Her mother and an aunt took care of her two children while she worked in the shoe factory. In her ethnic neighborhood, large families were common; they were the pride of the mothers and the boasts of the fathers. Concepta would occasionally stay out late and spend the evening in a bar, still eager to "meet the boys" before coming home. It was not until her third baby that she felt her life was pulling together. This father stayed with her, she switched to a part-time job, and she was content, "…just like the other women," she said with a smile.

Concepta's culture condoned the male's serial fathering of children out of wedlock and tolerated women's successive pregnancies. It also provided interim care for the children. Her image of motherhood included an initial period of indiscrete fecundity before settling down with a serious guy who assumed the responsibilities, as she would do hers. It was only after the birth of her third child that this image of motherhood was activated, fulfilled if you want, and Concepta could move on to the next stage of her own growth as an adult.

CHILDREN AS TEACHERS

Before we move to the next period in our lives with children, we can reach some conclusions already, to be confirmed in the following chapters. One is that our children have the undeniable role of teachers in our lives. Starting with the early signals around pregnancy and birth, this child-effect will remain there for all of us who want to experience it.

We tend to still see ourselves as parents, doing the teaching and raising of our children most of the time, from minor things to major moral problems. But when we look closely, as we have done so far, we see how rich the nonverbal vocabulary of the newborn is, and how he can employ it to get what he wants and needs. The baby fusses—the parent checks out the diaper. The baby cries—the mother readies breast or bottle. The baby gazes into our face—we melt with affection, coo, cuddle, smile and talk to the little one.

These very early interactions and mutual responses set the stage upon which gradually, a more complicated conversation will be built and future interactions will take place. Because the child is the most needy one at first, we perhaps tend to overlook the stream of signals that we get in return for all our labors. A major part of that stream, of course, are the many positive signals we get from the satisfied child: "You are a good person; you make me happy; I love you." But the mostly one-way interaction of parent and child is gradually replaced by a two-way exchange, and with effort and luck, it can become a true collaboration. An important role our children play in this exchange is that of teacher. We already saw a few examples in earlier chapters. Here I would like to emphasize only two more aspects in which our children nudge us along our journey through adulthood.

The first one is the cultivation of altruism:, the second of integrity. Altruism gets a strong boost during pregnancy, but it is often most keenly felt during the child's infancy. It is as if our species, too, is willing to set aside selfish concerns in order to increase the survival chances of the next generation. We get up in the middle of the night to comfort the crying child, and we sacrifice personal plans and leisure activities. We put the child's interests ahead of our own. We don't usually think of this as an exercise in altruism, as a step in our adult development. But we are making developmental progress. We prepare for maturity as we age. What may initially feel like a burden, turns out to be training for future developmental phases, particularly those Erikson called generativity, during which we redirect the altruism of parenthood to caring for the world at large. This, in turn, prepares us for the last stage: integrity. This is when we need to come to a sense of meaning in and for our life beyond ourselves.

A parent writes:

"Certainly my children have a pervasive influence on the way I live, with the obvious effect that my role has changed. Prior to children, I worked for perfection, personally and professionally. Now, post-children, I consider my purpose on this planet to be that of a support system for my children. Instead of individual attainment I seek to be a better parent. The major issue is knowing that my children will live on. This is a great comfort as signs of aging appear. My children give me a justification to let go. It's OK if I'm older and more flawed as an athlete, as a male, or as an intellectual, because, after all, I'm just a parent."

Newborn babies also induce us into the larger community of parents. The same parent writes:

"Children permeate the fabric of our life now. Unlike when we lived in Massachusetts, we know many of our neighbors because they have children. We have become aware of our friends' and relatives' child-rearing practices and have been drawn closer to those whose practices are similar to ours and felt dismay at those whose practices seem mean or thoughtless."

It is not difficult to see in this account the progression from self-interest to altruism, first for the child, then hinting at larger concerns beyond the family.

We have now finished looking down some of the paths these unborn or newborn children open up for us. They lead to goals that we, as parents and adults, need to reach on our journey: sustained intimacy, marriage, a loosening of the bonds with the previous generation, esteem for self and ownership of our lives, connection with others, altruism and the gradual relinquishing of power. The list is not exhausted. We have felt our joys renewed, the satisfactions earned, and we have seen how the scope of our adult life is enlarged. And all this amid diapers, broken toys, fever charts and piles of laundry!

We are now ready to turn to the preschool years with their own pitfalls and promises for adult growth.

CHAPTER FOUR

THE LEARNING PARENT:
PRESCHOOL YEARS

The parents exists to teach the child,
but also they must learn what the child has to teach them,
and the child has a very great deal to teach them
Arnold Bennett

As the baby becomes a toddler and grows into the preschool years, the developmental dance between children and parents becomes more energetic and complicated. The child begins to explore its world, itself, and us, its parents and we hear about the discoveries along the way. Up to now the child's influence on us was largely in the form of signals. From now on we can expect to see symbols and, with language enriching the communication, even some beginning sequences.

What else can we expect? Skirmishes around boundaries for one. We draw boundaries around our personal space to protect them. They are challenged by the child's explorations and increasingly autonomous movement. A child enters the "the terrible twos and threes" This means simply that we will be provoked into skirmishes and negotiations during which our and our children's boundaries, as well as our own, will be made clear. It means also that we have to face the problems of independence and discipline. The surging biological growth during the preschool years foreshadows the later questions of sexuality and gender. The child's cognitive growth makes its early contribution to moral development. All of these bring countless interactions with our children, promising rich material for us parents to experience, examine, ponder and draw conclusions. These conclusions can benefit our own self-understanding and growth.

From the examples of symbols and sequences in this chapter, we will see how some parents have used this period to their own rewards. These parents were willing to be taught by their children. They gained surprise insights and they reviewed their value systems. These parents paid attention to their children's doings and sayings as well as their own reactions, and they came out as winners. The preschool years may be testing our mettle, but there is no better training for our future.

Letting Your Child Teach You

Neal, a construction supervisor, had lived in the city all his life. He took its noises, colors and smells for granted when he walked through his neighborhood. When Jessica, his daughter, turned three, she began to accompany him. Now Neal's stroll took an hour. Jessica marveled at the store windows, stared at the passersby and bopped to the street band on the corner. One evening, Jessica spotted an anthill exposed in a sidewalk crack. For a few minutes they watched in delight at the ants' scurrying activities. For Neal, each evening walk became an adventure.

Learning from your child is a result of the child's symbolic message: "Look at this! I see something different! Maybe I am different from you, too!" and from the parent taking it seriously. Their responding to each other about a shared interest can start the kind of sequence common in these early years. The child's naivete and enthusiasm in seeing the world for the first time and commenting on its discoveries, can be a precious education for the listening parent. We encountered an example in chapter one, when my daughter showed me water coming out of a rock.

Educator Herbert Kohl refers to the toddler's fascination with the "why" and "how" of the world as the:

"contemplative component—the disinterested observing of the world; the wonder one sees in many children's faces when they see something new or beautiful. ...unfortunately, many parents become impatient with their children spending time observing. Observing, losing oneself in thought or in the sights and sounds of the world, leads to respect for things in the world, and a heightened capacity for love and joy."[xxi]

He adds, candidly, "It has taken many years for me to slow down enough to observe the world in that simple way."

By allowing ourselves to become a pupil and accompanying our children wholeheartedly on their journey of discovery, we relearn our own sense of wonder, optimism, and love—if we can remain perceptive. This recharges and refreshes us on our journey, burdened as we are by responsibilities at home and at work.

For those of us living in the fast lane, discovering the joy that comes from spending time to watch and listen to our children often inspires a shift in life's tempo. In this way, raising children can become increasingly rewarding, instead of stifling, despite restrictions on one's freedom and time. This process of change is almost never a one shot deal. (In this sense, some of the vignettes in this book could be misleading.) Profound changes more often occur in steps over time, years, or decades.

Juliette's change, under her daughter's influence, unfolds in a long series of events of which we shall give one example now, and others later. Juliette, a single and inexperienced mother, allowed her daughter Rhonda's influence to expand over the years from simple signals to the most generous sequence: collaboration.

Juliette sat next to an older woman on a park bench. Rhonda, then two years old, had just scampered a few steps away before she stumbled and fell. Juliette jumped up and ran to her. " Oh dear! Are you hurt?" Rhonda, alarmed by her mother's anxiety, burst into tears. Juliette soothed her in her lap until she calmed down.

When Rhonda had left her lap again the older woman said, "You know, when my son was a toddler I used to jump up every time he fell down until someone pointed out to me that it was I who was frightening him. When kids fall down and haven't really hurt themselves, they aren't sure how to react. They look at you to get a clue. If you look scared, they become scared too. If you just smile, they feel reassured."

The comment was new, but made sense to Juliette. As could be expected, Rhonda, exploring the playground, stumbled again. Curious to see what would happen, Juliette managed to remain calm. Rhonda looked at her with wide-open eyes, hesitated, and began to whimper. Juliette smiled at her, opened her arms and said, "Good! Nice fall! Mama is here!" Rhonda stopped whimpering, got up again, and continued her exploration.

This incident taught Juliette an important lesson. She had missed a crucial signal: her daughter's quizzical look at her after she fell. Parents' reactions to their children's mishaps shape their children's responses. Juliette's anxiety prompted Rhonda to cry when she fell down, even if nothing was wrong with her. Moreover, Juliette had learned that she had a choice in how to show concern for her daughter. She didn't need to jump up even if she felt the impulse to do so. She could control her responses. She could think first, then act. This approach also allowed

Rhonda more freedom; she could set her own pace and tone, instead of mimicking her mother's reaction.

This is a very early example of a symbol that was almost missed: "Look, Mama I fell! Am I OK?" It is also an example of how we parents can establish a pre-collaborative pattern of give-and-take with our children. Rhonda will let Juliette know if she really needs her or not. What Juliette decides to do then is more likely to be appropriate and helpful. Each has a choice in how to act. Together they will determine what happens. Family life is filled with events like this one where we can either behave impulsively, traditionally, or establish a thoughtful give-and-take.

Between the ages of two and five, children make stunning advances in motor skills: climbing, running, and skipping as well as threading beads or scribbling with a pencil. Intellectual growth, included in language and abstract thinking, is phenomenal. Social skills are learned and a sense of self and self-confidence emerge. Many parents are awed by this transformation of a small, babbling baby into a child who chatters nonstop, runs all day without a nap, argues passionately about what to eat or to wear, and asks questions with a hungry curiosity.

Boundaries and Limits

During this move into toddlerhood we have to move along also. Still reeling from the transition from self-involved adult without children, to caregiver with children, we are now challenged to answer all questions, account for every decision and provide guidance twenty-five hours per day!

As a child becomes more independent, stronger, and begins to roam around the house, we are alert and decide what the toddler can safely do. This new world of unlimited opportunities needs some structure. Can he play with scissors or matches? Can she climb down the stairs or cross the street? Will he taste the ammonia? Each time we interrupt a risky venture, the little one is frustrated and will show it through acquiescence, protest, rebellion, or by sneaking around it, and we have to face the music. For many of us this shift from loving caregiver to roving police is a thankless one to make, to say the least.

Phil—we met him already in Chapters One and Three—loved to take his little daughter, Eve, with him on his walks. He'd point out the minor miracles of a running rabbit, a spider web bejeweled with dew, or a hawk wheeling overhead. But sometimes Eve just wanted something else: the promised ice cream, going home, or to be carried. Then her asking could turn into whimpering, then whining and finally fortissimo wailing. At that pitch, and when his efforts to distract her had run out, he'd pick her up and carry her sometimes. "I love her," he'd say. "I can't stand her crying very well." Having soothed her, he'd put her back on her little feet. "Daddy gets tired of carrying you. You are a heavy four-year-old. You can walk a little bit now." Or he would say, "We are going back home, sweetheart." Soon she'd be running after a butterfly, or start all over again. "I can't always give in and I can't let her scream. It's hard."

Phil, we remember, helped raise his younger siblings. He also had become an expert at dog training. "I know you can't let them have their way because they'll run all over you," he said, commenting on his two rambunctious Labradors, "but you can't keep the leash too short either."

He had learned how to tread the fine line between frustration and indulgence; the tug for power when decibels and guilt face each other off. At times, when he knew Eve was tired or just getting over a cold, he'd carry her all the way home and she would fall asleep on his shoulder. Other times, he'd just let her sit and pout and wait her out until she'd caught up with him to continue their walk. Eve knew it was always him who decided. "I know when she gets too demanding that I've given in too much. When she really wants something, she does ask for it in a different way and I give it to her."

He had learned to pay attention to subtle clues from her, and would be guided by her reactions and her feedback. In the language of symbols, she was telling him if he was doing things right or not. "But, it's really hard, you know," he'd say. "You have to really know what's going on and pay a lot of attention. I don't see how people who don't spend enough time with their kids can do it."

This father had learned how to tolerate a frustrated child. He had learned not to deprive her of frustration either. He had learned from his experience, and from his daughter's reaction to him, that to remain credible as a parent, one can't let the child call the tune, nor can one become too harsh or restrictive. No one ever said it was going to be easy.

The "how to raise your child" books will swing the pendulum over time from permissiveness to discipline and back again, as each generation tries to improve on the previous one. It is precisely in this gray area in between, where we can be alerted by our kids as to how we are doing, as Phil did. This is when we really know what's going on and pay a lot of attention. Out of this give-and-take around setting limits between child and parent, grows a future collaborative mode. This father became a competent and reliable parent for his kids and for others. He felt good about what he was doing by watching them grow.

But doing this well is especially trying for parents who find it difficult to accept and set limits. Only a Mae West could proclaim that, "Too much of a good thing is...wonderful!" For those of us who raise kids, limits are the "restraint that dignifies the human condition," as William Trevor called them.[xxii] There's only so much they can do, want, expect, etc. By giving in too often, parents find themselves sucked into a quicksand of demands, decibels and drama. If this happens, and no other adult comes to the rescue, an observant parent will find in the child's behavior clues to grab for a slow way out.

Carol, a thirty-five-year-old teacher and single mother, found herself unprepared for her son's entry into toddlerhood. Before Nicky's birth, she had fantasized about what to accomplish during her maternity leave: get the house in order; read that stack of books. After eight months, Carol had written nine thank-you notes and read three chapters of one book. Efficient by nature, she was distraught at how disorganized she had become.

Carol had looked forward to the time when Nicky could walk, talk and be more of a companion. She had never anticipated the whirlwind of noise and activity of a three-year-old! He needed more supervision than before. To put the laundry in the dryer was risky. Who knew what he might get into? Nicky whined when she talked on the phone or tried to read. Taking him shopping meant constant questions and requests for toys and snacks. Parenthood had become a series of tests for Carol. She got irritable and wondered how she could continue. How could she evolve from slave to companion?

A friend set her on the trail, asking, "How come you can handle second graders, and not manage your own kid? Maybe Nicky is asking for something he is not getting?"

As a teacher, Carol had learned a few things in the classroom that she seemed to have forgotten with her child. She had forgotten that distraction often works, or promising a reward for good behavior. She could also offer an alternative of her choice: no ice cream now, but a red crayon later. When the new truck was instantly ruined, she noticed Nicky's fascination with the catalogue it came from, so she turned to picture books that were read together.

This mother had missed the symbolic message in her son's constant testing of the limits, which was, in our terms, a symbol. The message interpreted was: "When are you going to stop me, because I can't do it myself quite yet." A friend had started her in the process of looking beyond the immediate behavior of her son, where the answer to her questions lay. As she set limits with more ease and her son accepted them, she grew more confident as well.

The preschool years can wear us out. There is comfort in the thought that help is available (if we know how to find it) in the form of child-effects: from the very source, it seems, of our difficulties!

The toddlers begin to stake out their space and initiative as a sense of self emerges. They meet immovable limits in the realities of this world: the stove is too hot to touch; the ball too big to grasp; the bunny has claws. The toddler learns to live with them quickly. But in the probing of the more movable boundaries of the parent, it will pry for the limit to which it can push. Growth wants its way. Should you let her splash in the mud puddle? Should you let him watch the show knowing he'll be cranky missing his nap?

Deciding how much independence to foster, or how much initiative to tame, we parents can draw on the dos and don'ts we grew up with, and on how these lines were drawn for us. We saw a good example of this in Chapter Three, when a father had to deal with his son who dropped a muddy ball on the carpet of his grandmother. Her stern admonition was enough to remind him of his own pain at her hands and how not to draw that line. His reaction to the incident was different: he could monitor the activity of his son and his response to his mother, and better understand his relation to her in the process. In few other realms of life can we see so clearly that understanding truly gives power. This father was growing daily with his children.

"Discipline." The word alone tends to arouse strong feelings. Discipline can evoke the mind-numbing uniformity of goose-stepping soldiers, but also the expressive grace of the steps of a trained ballerina. Training to follow rules can be constrictive or liberating.

Discipline can be used as social control, as in a boarding school, but it can also be the means to channel human talent, as in any good school. As parents we have to navigate these two currents all the time, because we want our kids to learn the rules of society as well as make use of their potential to contribute to it. Since most societies are none too good at maintaining this balance, we can't fault ourselves too much for having a hard time with it.

As preschoolers assert their independence more and more, we have to steer this headlong rush and show how to transform anarchy into freedom; license into liberty.

The better we learned how to deal with our own early frustrations, the easier we can tolerate not being an all-giving, all-smiles, indulgent parent, and help our child come to terms with the limits we have to impose. Few parental responsibilities are as evocative of our own childhood experience as having to discipline our child. As we saw in Chapter Three, it leads to instant signals. In the preschool years we encounter symbols or even sequences resulting from our dealing with this dilemma.

A scene I have watched often in my own living room:

A child approaches the burning wood stove. Inquisitive, it reaches out for this novel source of warmth. The watchful parent jumps up and... does what? One parent will grab the child and pull it away, scolding it. But some of the child's curiosity remains and it tries again. The other parent will come close, ready to intervene, and stretch out their own hand slowly, to the limit of comfort, and the child can repeat it. A third will watch, perhaps call a warning, and risk the child's own experience to become its teacher.

The first parent, reacting on impulse, will get another chance, until its gets the symbol right. "My kid is doing something I have to help it with. I'd better start thinking how I can do that."

The second parent got the message from the symbol right away. But what to do? Yank her back? Let him get burned and find out? "I want him to find out, but…carefully. I have to restrain him somehow, but make it fun at the same time. How did I learn from my parents? Was it fun? Did I like it? Did I want them to do something different?"

The curious child provokes this kind of review in a perceptive parent and the parent's response will redefine their self-image. Even the impulsive parent may get a chance. The child asks, "Daddy, why do you get angry when I get hurt?" This then may be the start of a sequence, depending on how the parent takes it. The answer will tell the child something about risks and something about the parent.

Incidents like this will allow us to better understand how we act and make a change in our behavior. How we can do that step by step we can see in the next vignette:

One evening, shortly after Carol had told Nicky, her four-year-old, "No more ice cream," she spotted him cutting a sizeable hole in the screen door with a plastic knife. Carol couldn't believe her eyes. She shouted at Nicky, "Are you crazy? Why did you do that? That was a very bad thing to do!" Nicky just sat and stared at her, neither intimidated nor chastised by her anger. Yelling did nothing to alleviate Carol's anger. She grabbed him. "You just stay in your room until I call you." Then she took a few deep breaths and sat down to think.

How could she punish him? How could she make him understand what he had done? It was going to be expensive to get it fixed. Should he stay in his room? How unfazed he was as he just sat there staring at her, as if he were saying, "What's going on here? What's the matter with you?"

Carol tried to sort out why she felt so furious. She was unsure of how to discipline him and unsure of herself. She didn't want to traumatize him, but he should learn that what he had done was wrong. She decided to let Nicky out of his room after he had apologized—of sorts. At bedtime she talked to him about what he did and why it was not a good thing. He seemed to understand. Then she called her brother Rick.

Rick reminded her that she, the younger sister, had been "a model child" who rarely needed discipline. He, Rick, had needed it and got it. Carol was always terrified of their father's anger. Their mother had used disapproval as her tactic. Yes, Carol admitted, this fear of disapproval had haunted her life, often leaving her feeling helpless and insecure.

Although she had lashed out as her father might have done, Carol's hesitation stemmed from her unwillingness to repeat either her father's or her mother's pattern of discipline. She could see that now. By giving Nicky, and herself, time out, she had curbed the anger and diffused the situation. But what about the intense rage she had felt?

When she saw the large hole Nick had cut, she assumed he had retaliated for her refusal of ice cream. But was that it? How do you interrogate a four-year-old? Was it important to know why he did it?

Carol paid attention to the symbol her little boy had presented her with: "What's going on here? What's the matter with you?", as well as to her own feelings and musings. She came to realize that his behavior and seemingly nonchalant reaction to her anger, had made her feel threatened and out of control herself. Would he become a bad seed or a juvenile delinquent? Could or would she one day blow a fuse, as her father had done, and bully him? Were they a bad child and a bad parent?

She could have dismissed the whole incident, but she took into account her reaction, her impulses, her feelings and her brother's reminiscences. The incident brought her hazy memories into focus again. Caught between her father's intimidating anger and her mother's withering disapproval, she had felt powerless and enraged. Was she not a good mother? The anger was hers, not Nicky's. It fed her self-doubt. Yet, she had been able to take some distance from both extremes of rage and disapproval, cool off, and talk it out with her son. She could become angry, just enough, and not condemn herself for it. This helped her regain some sense of balance and self-respect, and increase the distance between herself and the parental examples. The incident was to be one in a series of interactions with her enterprising son that helped Carol become a more competent parent.

Once we figure out how not to make victims and how not be victimized ourselves by our responsibility as parents, we begin to see that parenthood is more than a challenge, it also brings unexpected profit to our lives. A true reward of parenthood indeed.

Don't we all know how we can get carried away by frustration or anger? Our kid can provoke us in an unguarded moment, having learned already how to use our weak spots. We may loose our cool, shout and say things we don't really mean, or we become violent. But even in these extremes, the voice of our child is still able to call us back from the brink, as long as we can still hear it.

<u>*Even If You Weren't My Father*</u>

Father, even if you weren't my father,
were you an utter stranger,
for your own self, I'd love you.
Remembering how you saw, one winter morning,
the first violet on the wall across the way,
and with what joy you shared the revelation:
then, hoisting the ladder on your shoulder,
out you went and propped it to the wall.
We, your children, stood watching at the window.

And I remember how, another time,
you chased my little sister through the house
(pigheadedly, she'd done I know not what).
But when she, run to earth, shrieked out in fear,
your heart misgave you,
for you saw yourself hunt down your helpless child.
Relenting then, you took her in your arms
in all her terror: caressing her, enclosed in your embrace
as in some shelter from that brute
who'd been, one moment since, yourself.

Father, even if you were not my father,
were you some utter stranger,
for your innocence, your artless tender heart,
I would above all other men
so love you.[xxiii]

Can it be said in a more moving way? Here was a moment of grace. A furious father could see himself through the eyes of his child. Even in his rage, he did hear her terror. The restraint that dignifies the human condition was aroused, and we read about the effect of this incident on the daughter and the affirmation of her love for him. Can you now imagine the thrill the father must have felt; his jubilant triumph of having bettered his anger and won the love and respect for himself?

We also begin to see the outlines of what we need to do to reap this welcome harvest, looking at the parents who have been described so far. It seems to have to do with a certain willingness to suspend the knee-jerk reaction. Self-control? It also seems to require a genuine willingness to listen to and take seriously what the child says and does. Receptive openness? In most of our examples, the parent took time to think things through, and to let the mind wander to other feelings and memories The parent thought of times when he or she was in the same predicament as a child. Musing on the past and present events play a role. We will have more to say about this in Chapter Eight.

Besides boundaries, limits and discipline, the preschooler's parent will have to contend with emerging independence. Closely related are: gender-identity, sexuality, and moral development. We shall now spend some time on these, keeping in mind that our focus is on how parental development will be affected by the child.

INDEPENDENCE

We saw in Chapter Two, Erikson describing toddlerhood as a stage in which children begin to develop a sense of autonomy (independent selfhood); for preschoolers the task is one of initiative. Both involve further degrees of moving away from the parent, which allows for another kind of relatedness than the complete dependence the child has had so far. Carol Gilligan believes that achieving separation and independence are not universally important developmental tasks. "For boys and men," she says, "separation and individuation are critically tied to gender separation, since separation from the mother is essential for the development of masculinity. For girls and women, issues of feminine identity do not depend as much on the achievement of separation from the mother or the process of individuation. Masculinity is defined more through separation while femininity is defined more through attachment."[xxiv]

Nevertheless, as little boys and girls experiment with their newly found physical strength, verbal skills and social confidence, they are beginning to separate themselves out from their parents. A new world seems to open up for them and it is filled with goodies now within their grasp. It is the difficult time of: "I want to..." and the often necessary: "sorry, you can't yet..." A new set of restrictions replaces the ones just overcome. To the child, this is frustrating.

How does a parent strike a balance between spoiling (too few frustrations) and deprivation (too many)? We already saw some of this dilemma tackled by parents in "setting limits." Understanding and coping with your child's vocal assertiveness and healthy push for independence can be achieved with skill and subtlety. But how we, as parents, can derive a secondary benefit from this process, an unexpected prize for all our efforts and anxieties, is rarely made clear. As we shall see in the next vignettes, we have to be patient, introspective, and responsive to our inner stirrings.

Usually a child wants more or tries to attempt more than it can handle. Let's see how one father dealt with this dilemma, and what he gained from it. The father writes:

"When Paul was two years old, he occasionally liked to help out at mealtimes. At lunch one Saturday, my wife was out doing errands so I made sandwiches for Paul and me. Paul was contributing by getting a jar of pickles out of the refrigerator and bringing it to me. But when he hoisted it up to the table, it fell and broke into pieces, spreading pickles, juice and glass all over the floor. I grabbed him quickly to see if he had been cut and carried him away to clean him off. He was unhurt and mildly upset. I remember thinking that this was the kind of incident that would have enraged my father. He would have been so angry, he would have spanked me. I thought how trivial it was to clean up the mess! Why was it so big a problem for my father? My father must have operated with great pressure and virtually no reserve of patience to be so easily made distraught. I told Paul that he should be more careful the next time, but that it was OK, it was an accident. He hadn't been fooling around and I was surprised to find myself totally lacking in anger. Paul was initially concerned: it was a major but interesting event. He had been told glass could be dangerous, but he didn't seem to need any further reassurance and it all blew over quickly.

Many months later, Paul dropped a juice glass on the floor and it shattered. I came over quickly to pick it up before he got out of his chair, and told him to be more careful (in a slightly annoyed voice), because he had been fooling around with it. He quickly said, "It was just an accident! It's OK; everybody makes accidents sometimes." The way he said it let me know that he understood breaking glass was regrettable; his mistake.

I remembered how terribly important it always was for me to believe that my flaws and everything about me, was normal. I told him, "Yes, we all have accidents, but we try to be careful to avoid them." I felt proud that I could let him off the hook so gracefully, leaving him only with a small amount of remorse, in scale with the event."

These incidents reminded this father of similar mishaps when he was a child, and of his father's explosive responses and the burden that put on him. In therapy he had removed most of that burden. What was needed now was life experience to help him integrate the learned with the lived, and settle the old account, so he could emerge with a less punitive and judgmental attitude himself. It was little Paul who gave the symbol ("Don't get angry…it was an accident…I'm still learning"), providing an object lesson, so he could use the surprise insight and meet his goal of the "good enough" parent, ready to move on to the next adult steps he had to take. The groundwork for future sequences, including cooperation, had been laid.

He had not always been as introspective and responsive to his inner stirrings. Perhaps his therapy led him in that direction. Most parents do not have this kind of training, but they can learn to look at themselves and listen to what goes on inside themselves to have an inkling of how the child's actions makes them feel, and how that resonates with their own experience, and take it from there. An example:

Sarah, a thirty-eight-year-old chef at an upscale restaurant, remembers the day she and her husband moved their three-year-old son from his crib to the big boy's bed. "There I was, trying to reassure a crying Max that he would be fine in his great new bed when I just felt like crying myself. I couldn't quite figure out why. I loved Max as a baby, but I also loved watching him grow up and turn into a great little kid. I knew that an era was over. I would never be twenty-nine again, Max would never be two again, and I would never be a new mother again."

When Sarah went in that first night to check on Max, the bed seemed huge and Max looked tiny under the covers. Sarah sat down in the nearby rocking chair, musing over some of the earlier steps she and Max had taken together: the anticipation in setting up the nursery, bringing Max home, and the intimacy of nursing him. Then, just a week ago, watching Max dress himself for the first time.

Pondering all this, she also recalled how each step had its own difficulty: the anxiety before and the exhaustion after Max's birth, the mess when he moved from bottle to cup, and the patience she needed to let him dress by himself. Yet all these they had overcome together, and Max's, and her own, confidence grew. Each time she had to encourage herself, and him. Each time she and he had to give up what they had cherished for the gain they enjoyed.

Max stirred in his sleep. Sarah tucked him in and left, less wistful and more assured of the good she could be looking forward to.

This mother was intuitively tuned in to her son's crying and her own wistfulness. She took time to ponder their emotional reactions to the same event, and then looked back on other losses and gains for the benefit of both of them.

We have already seen what kind of reward parents can get when they grow along with their children. But when the parents, for whatever reason, lack the receptive openness needed for this influence, they will miss out on the enhancing effect. In that case, their own adult development will lack an important vitamin and it may stagnate, as the following vignette demonstrates.

The push for independence in a growing child is inevitable. It enables the individual to ultimately survive without its parents. But some parents whose attachment to their children does not evolve and grow along with this independence, become, themselves, dependent on their children, needing their kid's dependence on them for their own sense of worth. It can be truly difficult for these parents, or even painful, to see "their baby" move gradually away on its own drumbeat. They do little to encourage this process and get little in return.

Gabrielle had always been an energetic girl. She stood out in confirmation class for her inquisitive comments. She wanted to learn Spanish in high school, and play an instrument. After graduation she wanted to move to the big city. For her parents, small grocery store owners in a rural town, all this was unheard of and outright alarming.

Here was a girl who seemed bent on breaking the mold. Father refused to buy her a clarinet; Mother talked her out of Spanish courses. Gabrielle's efforts at shaping her own life were discouraged or opposed; she could not lock the bathroom door nor even her own room. The teacher who complimented the parents on her grades was told, "She's been reading too many books! She could've helped out more in the store!"

Gabrielle prevailed. She did not cave in, but blazed her own trail with a burden of shame and guilt for her disloyalty. Her parents remained insistent. All her initial troubles in the big city were blamed on her. "You could've stayed home!" they said. Their contacts withered. With some help, Gabrielle began to prize her hard-fought achievements in study and career. However, her parents remained bitter and frustrated, angry at what they saw as their abandonment by Gabrielle, still trying to tell her what to do; coming unbidden for visits, sending her food she did not need.

These parents had been unable to join their child in her dance toward autonomy. Consequently, the child-parent relationship had not evolved, but remained stuck in an early phase of parenting although the child was now fully grown. They were behind in their parental development and left out of their child's life. They now missed out on an essential ingredient required for sustained adult growth: the effect of the child. Child-effects are the vitamins in our parental diet; we can't go for long without them.

Gender Identity and Sexuality

Our era exploits sexuality for advertising or entertainment. Being sexually active is considered a badge of honor in many circles. Yet many parents feel an embarrassment at their own children's emerging sexuality.

Toddlers and preschoolers are wonderfully curious and open about sex. They are also sensual and affectionate. A child's naive and insistent questions about babies, birth and marriage, challenge the parent. In addition, a major task for preschoolers is understanding and establishing their gender identity. In trying to find out what is a boy and what is a girl, they force parents to explain not only how the world works, but also, if the parent aspires to gender equivalence , how they would like the world to be.

Gary, a thirty-three-year-old businessman, was raised in a traditional, conservative home. He does not remember his parents discussing sex or sexuality. When his mother told him she was having a new baby she called it a "blessed event." One incident stood out in Garry's sexual education. One morning, when he was about five, he ran into his parents' bedroom. He did not know that his pajama's had gotten twisted around, exposing his genitals. His mother, seeing this, exclaimed: "Cover yourself up! Don't you know better than to go around looking like that?" Gary was deeply embarrassed.

He would remember his mother's disapproving comment. It stood for a host of other memories, and for an atmosphere of alienation from the sensual and suspicion of bodily experience. Gary had been shy taking part in athletic activities, and during the time he was dating. He was awkwardly self-consciousness with his wife, even in their intimate moments.

Gary enjoyed having a son, but every time he changed Todd's diaper, he felt a little queasy. When he bathed Todd, he watched Todd touch his penis playfully. Gary caught himself wanting to tell his son to stop, but he didn't want to embarrass his son or make him self-conscious, so he remained silent.

When Todd was in kindergarten, he started asking his father

questions about anatomy. Several times he inquired: "How come my peewee gets bigger sometimes?"

Gary was at a loss for words. He would try to change the subject or say, "You'll find out when you are older."

Gary wanted his son to like being a boy and he wanted to be a good father. He decided to do something about his discomfort. He talked with Todd's pediatrician about what to say, and he read a few childcare books on the subject. The next time he gave Todd a bath, he was ready. Gary had a talk with Todd about body parts, the difference between boys' and girls' anatomy, and the need for privacy.

After this conversation with his son, Gary was relieved. Since he had mentioned his childhood experiences with sex in conversations with his wife, he did not have a dramatic moment of cathartic insight. He was able to replay his childhood events in another way. Now he understood his mother's discomfort. Gary could even recall some of his own excitement about his penis getting stiff and feel the pride that came before the shame. But by providing a better guidance for Todd, he had broken with the tradition of his parents. He had crossed over to the side of his son, who so clearly had shown him that sexual feelings in childhood are innocent, and that curiosity about sex is as much to be accepted as curiosity about any other aspect of life.

The son's curiosity and the father's embarrassment had been a symbol. With a smile, the boy had kicked open a door that his daddy, as a boy, had closed red-faced. With some help, this father had the courage to engage his kid in a sequence. With that, they had entered into a collaborative pact: the father put a lingering childhood shame behind him and allowed his son to feel no shame about his physical nature. Together, they grew up a little.

Helping girls and boys grow up in comfort with their sexuality is hard enough. To raise them believing that the genders should be valued the same, is heroic. Many parents today find themselves in the awkward situation of defending gender-equivalence in a world that is all but convinced of it. Boys are still thought of as rambunctious and tough (strong), while girls are considered demure and soft (weak). A girl dressed in blue is acceptable, but a boy dressed in pink?

Nevertheless, toddlers and preschoolers are eager to categorize themselves as either male or female. They often welcome stereotypes as a way of making the distinction easier.

A mother remembers giving her daughter a toy Jeep to play with. "It sat in her room, untouched. When we got her a dump truck, she folded a blanket in the back and made it a bed for some dolls." Later, a similar attempt to get her son interested in dolls also backfired. "I gave him three baby dolls to play with, suggesting they were brothers and sisters. A few minutes later, I overheard him playing war. The doll siblings were shooting at each other." She settled for stuffed animals, building kits, books and games either child would, and did, play with.

We often dutifully try to modify the still prevailing current in society that maintains gender stereotyping and unfair treatment for men and women. In this noble effort our children can assist us if we listen to their unselfconscious remarks. Our child may notice inequalities within our own family that we had been barely aware of.

One five-year-old boy, who had recently seen a TV show about the Civil War, watched his father at the dinner table being served by his wife. When the father asked her during the meal to answer the phone, and after dinner to bring him his glasses and newspaper, the budding scholar wondered: "Daddy, why do you ask

Mommy to be your slave?" Both parents were startled and only mildly amused, but secretly the mother felt somewhat vindicated. Her son had noticed something about the inequity of the workload at home. She wished her husband had been as perceptive. Now both were made aware of it.

The innocent question became a symbol for the parents of a larger issue between them. Their son's remark triggered an ongoing review between the spouses, and in time they did adjust to a more convincing example of gender equivalence at home.

Moral Development

When we make choices between good, better and wrong, we need some kind of standard to guide our choices by. For these we draw from morals and ethics, whether we are aware of it or not.

Toddlers are egocentric, despite their growing awareness of others. They see themselves as the center of the universe. According to Piaget children between two and seven are pre-operational: instead of using deductive logic, they make judgments based on their perception, experiences or events.[xxv] Habits and behaviors frowned upon by adults, such as stealing, lying or being rude, come naturally to toddlers. We take an active part in teaching our children what we consider virtuous and what we deplore.

What our children do or say, and our responses to it, lead us into an interaction or a discussion involving values. We are responsible. These kinds of sequences often begin in the pre-school years. As we help our children develop their sense of values (morality), our own comes inevitably into focus. There is our chance to re-examine and re-define our own morals. Whether it is explaining fairness to a preschooler, choosing which holidays to celebrate, or answering questions about death, the process of setting standards and teaching right and wrong invites us to state our moral position and stimulate our moral development.

Looking back at Carol's dilemma after Nicky cut the big hole in the screen door, we see how she had wondered if he was a "bad seed." Would he become a playground bully? Would he torture animals or be a juvenile delinquent? And how would that reflect on her? She wanted to do the best she could by him.

Parents like Carol, who feel responsible for their children, know that the seed of their children's future is contained in the parents' past, since the parental values are reflected in their children.

We affirm the traditions of our families, we ignore them, or we modify them.

The father we have met before writes again:

"Paul was barely three years old and curious about everything. I was watching him from a few feet away as he found his way into Grandpa's kitchen and began fiddling with the under-the-counter doors. Grandpa noticed it and became agitated, saying to both of us: "Keep him out of there! He's heading for mischief."

I picked up Paul, saying to Grandpa: "It's your house, so we will restrain him. At home we let him roam and explore more."

Grandpa's reply was, "Yes. but it's so much work to keep him from handling the wrong things if you let him wander around."

I thought to myself, well, he's right in a way. It is indeed less effort for the parent to disallow whole activities than to let kids poke around and keep track of all their moves. So his rules for me, when I was a child, were in place for his convenience, not because I was a bad boy, a natural troublemaker or just to save me from harm! I was not allowed to touch his tools because I would've made a mess or broken something, he used to say. As a parent I can sympathize with the need to avoid aggravation and to economize on effort, but I still think that, whenever possible, I'll let Paul try out all sorts of things, short of the truly dangerous ones, without making him feel he's doing something wrong. At times my parents think that my wife and I are too liberal in our childrearing practices, but my experience in life and in therapy have taught me that a long leash is better than a short one. I believe that in the long run our path will even be less burdensome, because there will be less built-in resentments and guilt to deal with in the years to come. Our children may enjoy the grace that comes with the feeling of self-empowerment.

Toddlers and preschoolers develop the beginning of a conscience and concern for others, feeling guilty when they do something wrong, begin to judge when something is fair or unfair, and empathize with others.

The same father writes about an incident that combines both the notion of wrong, guilt, and empathy.

"Only a week ago, I was working in the garden when my son sprayed me with the hose by mistake (some people think we're crazy to let him play with the hose, but he has loved it for his whole life and as I said, we're fairly liberal about things like that). I was tired, rushed, and somewhat frustrated, and lost my temper worse than I ever have with him. I grabbed the hose and deliberately swung it around to spray a line across his shirt. Paul was surprised and then furious, kicking a nearby toy saying: "I'm going to break this thing!" Then, with his feelings hurt, he ran across the yard and up a path to the edge of our territory, stopping there to cry. I felt terrible, and after a few seconds ran after him. I picked him up and brought him back, explaining that I was sorry, and that I wasn't supposed to spray him even if he had sprayed me first. I told him I was in a bad mood, so I had gotten angrier than I should have, and that I was sorry again. I made a mistake. He seemed to recover almost fully over the next five minutes and shortly we were working in the front yard as if nothing had happened. Afterwards, I talked about the incident with my wife, since I was still feeling remorseful. In retrospect, it seemed that telling him that I was wrong and that he didn't deserve to be sprayed helped him recover. I may have been more disturbed than he was about it. In reviewing the incident, I find that I am falling short of my goal of sainthood as a parent, but I suspect that may not be crucial to my children as long as I can be as good as I usually am as a parent."

We recall the incidents with the muddy ball and the jar of pickles this same father reported. Mindful of his own experience with critical and punitive parents, he decided not to call his boy "bad"—a moral condemnation he had suffered himself. Instead, he decided to focus on the act, not the actor, calling it a "beautiful mess", an "accident", or a "mistake"- just as it is said that God hates the sin but loves the sinner. This sequence between Paul and his dad shows us how a parent can come to terms with not having practiced what he preached, and, having forgiven his son, then moves on to forgive himself. The son provided only the incident to practice it in, and the symbol (crying, anger, running away) showed how he rejected the father's retaliation and felt aggrieved and angry. But see how they end up and how the father solidified once more the distance he had moved from a life-long preoccupation with a "bad" self-image and not letting it stymie his growth as a father.

So far we have seen sequences occur in a carefully prepared climate. This is an atmosphere where the child is seen as an entity apart from birth with its own rights and as time goes on, with its own obligations. This is where respect is shown for the child's otherness and opinion, its strivings and growing independence, where its feelings are taken as seriously as its words, and where contribution to the family, friends, and schoolmates, is acknowledged.

In this climate, the parent-child interaction can be open and mutually beneficial. If this sounds like a climate controlled room you are right. The picture is too idyllic, of course, but it is the ideal for which we strive. As parents, *we know* all too well that we often miss that mark and have to try harder next time. We won't attain sainthood in this life!

Celebrating holidays, for instance, requires us to come to terms with our religious beliefs. It is not easy to explain these sacred stories to our children in their language. How many of us returned to church or synagogue when our kids were ready for some kind of religious instruction? Our children compel us to talk about our beliefs in a child-friendly way.

"How do you make a baby? Where is God?" We have to define our values in response to their questioning, resisting the temptation to ignore it or to give a reply that turns them off. Although it is not always practical to answer this curiosity immediately, our preschoolers provide ample opportunity for us to examine our own morals, as we shall see below.

Tim, a young house painter, liked a good bargain. With a sale or a coupon, he thought he could beat the system. Although scrupulous with his own customers, he did not ask for a recount if he was given too much change in the store. "Losing petty cash won't hurt their profit," he'd say. He also pocketed an occasional packet of gum without paying. And, of course, he did not report all his income to the IRS. To Tim, these minor transgressions didn't count.

Tim took another line, however, when talking to his children. "It doesn't matter what you have done," he told four-year-old Brenda, "it only matters that you tell the truth."

One day he took Brenda and her three-year-old sister to the zoo. He asked for one adult admission and two half-price tickets for "under four." Brenda had just turned four one month ago, but he knew she would pass. Brenda, however, was proud of her age. She piped up, "Daddy, I'm four!" Tim tried to quiet her. The more he hushed her, the louder Brenda became. Finally he fumbled in his pocket and paid the cashier.

Inside the zoo, Tim took Brenda aside. "Don't ever do that to me again!" he said angrily. "Just go along with what I say, OK?"

Brenda was stunned for a moment. Tears filled her eyes. "OK, Daddy, but I was only telling the truth like you said. Why are you angry at me?"

"Yes, sweetheart," Tim said, his anger fading, "Don't worry about it. You're too young to understand. Let's have a nice time now."

The next day Tim reported the incident to his wife. He insisted he was right. Brenda would have to learn the ways of the real world when she was older. His wife was not too sympathetic. She didn't blame Tim for trying to skimp on the price, but she thought he'd set a bad example for the kids. "How can we expect them to be honest if we're not?" she wondered. They both agreed that the simple lesson, always tell the truth, wasn't so simple after all. How could they have a double standard, one for them, and one for the kids, on such a basic thing as honesty? What was more important, saving a few dimes or being honest?

This early sequence between Tim and Brenda led to a series of conversations. Both parents had been made aware of a very common dilemma in our moral attitudes. Brenda initiated some needed parental soul-searching. With each other's help, and more sequences like this one, they strengthened their moral sense and took steps towards a practicable value system they all could live by.

How do I raise my child? What is permissible and what is not? We have to make up our minds nonstop. Often we do this by knee-jerk, outside of our awareness. We may be on target, or it does not fit with the standards we want to be judged by. In the meantime the formation of our values takes place.

A child holding onto a toy which is not his own needs to learn to make the distinction between "mine" and "thine." When that is difficult to do, we can hear the echoes of how we learned that lesson. If we have little or no bad feelings associated with it, we can be kind, firm and supportive of this necessary frustration. If this is not the case, we may see something like the following incident.

Eddy had eagerly awaited his fifth birthday party because Keith, his best buddy, would come from across town. Eddy's mother, Grace, had planned games and a picnic. During the party, Eddy and Keith were inseparable, sharing their toys. As the afternoon drew to a close and parents came to pick up their kids, Eddy's father, Drew, came home in time to witness Keith's parting. Eddy was clutching Keith's favorite toy, a big plastic fire truck. Keith wanted it back, "It's mine, Eddy! Give it back!" No deal. Eddy clung to it silently. Drew felt acutely that he had to do something. But what? Please his guest or his son, whose birthday he had largely missed? "Come on, Eddy. Keith has to go home now. You can play with your dumpster," he said lamely. Eddy didn't budge. Then, suddenly, Eddy bolted, fire truck and all, with Keith in hot pursuit. Drew stood paralyzed.

Grace came up to Keith's mother. "We haven't seen you for a while, and Eddy has missed Keith a lot. I hope you can stay just a little longer and have a piece of the cake? I'll run and make some tea." They sat down to chat and were quickly joined by two curious little boys, each carrying the other's truck.

"Can we have some cake, too?"

Grace drew the two to her and said, "Do you think that the fire truck would like to stay here for a week and Eddy's dumpster can go home with Keith? Next Wednesday, when we come to visit, you guys can swap them again?"

The boys' faces dropped. Slowly they exchanged their cherished possessions. The bosom buddies parted excitedly. "See you soon!", they yelled.

Later that evening, Drew said, "That was a tough moment. I couldn't take the truck away and I couldn't let Eddy have it either."

"I could see it, honey," said Grace. "It was make or break for you. But you didn't grow up with older siblings. I had to share and let others have my toys all the time."

Drew thought for a few moments. "I guess so. How do you think they solved it by themselves?"

Grace answered, after a pause, "I think Eddy couldn't let go of the truck because he couldn't let go of his friend. When they were together again, they shared, and each had a piece of the other. So when I gave them a choice, they opted for each having his own."

Drew laughed and said, "You're clever. I used to get upset when other kids came to play and use my toys. My mother got annoyed at me for hoarding them, or crying when something broke. So I didn't want to yell at Eddy, not on his birthday. I felt awful just looking at him cuddling that truck. I couldn't think of a way to let him know he couldn't keep what wasn't his. I'm glad you were around!".

Grace concluded:" Maybe you felt you had to do something that instant. But the boys weren't through yet. All they needed was a little more time and to be let off the hook. I learned early that things can work themselves out with maybe just a little nudge."

This father was blocked from playing the judge-on-call by having learned too well that holding on to one's toys was "wrong," sharing them was "right," and not to do what was right, was very wrong. He wanted badly to do right by his son and his son's friend, but in his confusion, got stuck, and couldn't pay attention to his son's silent, symbolic message which might have helped him: "I'm not yet ready to let go of my playmate!" Seeing how his wife, who had no such qualms, dealt with it, and how the kids resolved it when given the chance, was for him an object lesson in compassion and judgment.

This parent wavered between indulging his child, and coming down hard on him, and in so doing repeating his parents' insensitivity. In either case, this either/or father would not be acting according to the values he liked to foster. This unease prepared him for a symbol his son presented him with: "Look Dad, it's not the truck I want. We can share, OK?" After his wife's relation - oriented perspective on the symbol, he was able to take a close and beneficial look at himself.

"Our best users of language, poets and lovers and children and saints, use words to make: make intimacies, make character, make beauty, make truth,"[xxvi] wrote a wise theologian. Where adults fail, it pays to listen to the children. Toddlers and preschoolers frequently act as checkpoints, observing our behavior and commenting on it with uncanny accuracy. When we can come to terms with ourselves as authorities, endure our children's attempts at independence and support their curiosity, we will find ourselves challenged as well as refreshed. Our own development will be facilitated and our burden lightened. This welcome reward from parenthood deepens as our children move into the next phase of their school years, when the interactions with them create new challenges and offer new rewards.

CHAPTER FIVE

THE RELAXED PARENT:
GRADE SCHOOL

> *King Agesilaus II of Sparta was seen to be riding his horse*
> *early one morning with his young son seated in front of him.*
> *They came upon an astounded slave working a field.*
> *The farmer stood perplexed.*
> *The king asked, "What are you staring at, man?"*
> *"Sire," answered the poor chap, "I'm not accustomed to seeing you*
> *riding so early, alone, and with a little boy!"*
> *"Do you have children?", the king wanted to know.*
> *"No, Sire," was the answer.*
> *The king got ready to leave, turned around and said,*
> *"This little boy is my son. When you have children,*
> *you'll know why I enjoy this,*
> *and you will not be amazed anymore!"[xxvii]*

It is rare to find such an intimate and credible anecdote involving a child in classical literature. The mythologies of Ancient Greece, the Nordic countries, India, Persia and China, as well as the Bible, give examples of children "saving" their elders, often by knowing or being able to do something these elders can't. This may reflect a universal awareness that intuitive wisdom, such as that of the child, has saving potential.

This royal anecdote survived twenty-three centuries, thanks to its improbability. Kings would not go about unaccompanied and boys were left in the care of the women until puberty, when they were inducted into manhood. For parents to claim that raising a child was enjoyable, was simply unheard of!

Times have changed. Now we consider this period of childhood, the school-age years from about five to twelve, usually enjoyable for parents. It is also a period of our own childhood which we can remember and often with pleasure.

Language helps our memory—events and feelings have names. Many of us can tell funny or exciting stories from that time or recall names of childhood friends. These years are a joy compared with the overall unpredictability and constant turmoil of early childhood, the demands of babies, the struggles with toddlers and preschoolers, as well as the powerful "Sturm und Drang" (tempest and tension) of adolescence. Our child needs neither constant supervision nor does it need to be liberated from us. Instead, it is preoccupied with activities and interactions that fall mainly outside the parental sphere: the street, the buddies and friends, the first clubs or organizations to be joined, and school. It is the time to begin the turn towards the outside world; to rely on peers for company and comfort; to learn the social skills and the necessity of work; and to acquire knowledge about the world that is independent of the home. Erikson called the main task for this period, "industry," and pointed out that children learn the basic "technology of the tribe." (Clearly, he wrote this before the time when we learned the latest computer tricks from our kids!)

In this stage, children are more articulate. We can understand them better; there is less need for translating signals or interpreting symbols. Their bodies and feelings change less dramatically and the growth of their thinking capabilities is easier to follow.

This "golden age of childhood" often coincides with a period of relative calm in our own lives as parents and adults. (It is also called latency, though I could not find much latent in it). In the span from ca. 30-45, the family is often established, the career has taken shape, social life is consolidated, and the marriage, if it is good, enjoys a period of increased intimacy. For us, too, there is a calm before the storm. After the giddy early years of marriage and family life and before the coming roller coaster of midlife transitions, we can feel confident and can relax (a bit).

However, the transition to school age and the turn to the world was more joyful for King Agesilaus than it turns out for some of us:

A young father and mother were driving home after bringing their son to his first summer camp. It was a bright day. The sun lavished light over the wooded hills and valleys, but the father drove as if he was heading for a dark storm: sullen and staring in the distance. He had been less than enthusiastic about letting the kid go, but the boy had been happily anticipating the new adventure. Suddenly, he broke out in tears and stopped the car. His wife gently put her hand on his arm. "It's not easy, is it?" He began to recall his own childhood separations forced upon him for different reasons, and his despair each time when his parents left; his desolation when they were gone. "But they left you, darling. Our boy was ready to go."

He began to see and experience the fortunate difference between the two partings. They left their son chatting with the other boys in his cabin, while he could still see himself sitting, mute, in an empty room. This separation was not the tragedy that it seemed to him as a child. It had strained the bond between him and his parents, while his kid loved the camp. He used this signal-experience to re-work his old problem in the light of adulthood with its stronger supports, increased experience, and better grasp of the real world. Over the summer and beyond, the father became supportive of his son's excursions away from home, and their relationship remained firm.

While our kids enjoy the ride from early childhood to adolescence, we jog from early parenthood to midlife (also compared to a "second adolescence"). Settled in the world as we are, we introduce our kids to it, teaching the "technology of the tribe," (the basic skills to enter that world) with Eriksonian industry. During this transit they are by no means shy to give a running comment on this education and on us. Signals will still be there, like the loose tooth, the first report card, or a sleepover. These signals will remind us of our own developmental steps and what they came to mean for us. The experience of the crying father, described above, is such an example. Our kids will also use symbols to communicate, especially when they can't directly tell us what is on their minds. If we have done well by them so far, we will see in this stage an increase of sequences, which, once they are regular fare, can help to smooth a rocky path through the thickets of adolescence. In the following we shall focus on these child-effects, mainly those occurring around the major activities of this period: socialization and education—friends and schools. This does not imply that sexual, moral, or spiritual development stagnates from age five to twelve, but that they are less prominent in these years.

The Child at School

Since school is the defining element of this period, let us look at a few typical situations that can have a formative effect on parents.

When we bring our child to school, the two of us pass a major milestone in our lives hand-in-hand. Experiences at school can have a profound effect on a child's sense of confidence and self-worth. School can be, after all, a place of crushing losses and glowing successes. Guiding our child through these rapids will be a demanding but rewarding parental responsibility. As for us, child psychologist Bruno Bettelheim describes the impact of a child entering school on the parents:

"… our anxieties about entering school have stayed with us; in fact, some people spend a lifetime demonstrating to themselves, much more than to others, that their childish fears of academic and social failure were unrealistic… Efforts to understand the role played by parallel events in our own development always bring about beneficial changes as they provide new clarity about ourselves. We gain a deeper understanding of what certain experiences have meant in our lives and in relation to our parents. Such understanding permits us to empathize with our child, and this nearly always gives our relation greater depth and meaning, making it a more enjoyable experience for both of us. Thus, around some common experiences, we not only influence our child's attitude, but we also change our own, because of a better understanding of what similar events meant to us as children".[xxviii]

What Bettelheim here calls a "parallel event" is the similarity of an event in the child's life to one remembered by the parent. We have seen some parallel events in Chapter Four, and called them "replays." When our child faces a situation we once had to face ourselves it becomes a replay. If the kid has trouble with it, we are in a position to help somehow. If the child manages it better than we did, we can be inspired to review how we missed the boat and perhaps begin to correct for it. If it seems like a threshold we both stumbled over, we are getting an unmistakable signal that some work needs to be done. Let us now look at another of these "replay effects" of a parallel event.

Deborah, a thirty-seven-year-old mother of two children ages three and six, was a successful manager in a clothing store and accustomed to having her way. Her first elementary school conference for her daughter Megan, however, was a humbling experience. Facing Ms. Parker, who looked no more than twenty-eight, Deborah felt small and powerless. Even if she managed to convince Ms. Parker that Megan was smart and special, she knew that her daughter was only one of twenty-four children in the classroom. Her needs might go unnoticed or unrecognized. Deborah found herself babbling about how nice the room looked and how much Megan liked Ms. Parker. All the skills and confidence Deborah had learned as an adult seemed to have dissolved, to be replaced by a little girl that she barely recognized.

Recounting her feelings to her friend Margie the next day, Deborah laughed at her discomfort. With Margie's help, she thought about what she could do in the future to feel less intimidated. She knew Megan had a good year in kindergarten. She liked Ms. Parker and enjoyed class activities. Although Deborah wanted to be vigilant about Megan's schooling, she recognized Megan was capable of learning how to be part of the class, relate to Ms. Parker, and speak up when necessary.

What had happened here? Deborah was back in an elementary school classroom facing a teacher. She hadn't been in this situation for at least thirty years, but it brought back the overpowering emotions she had felt as a little first-grader. She felt small and powerless with a need to please the teacher. It was a perfect replay! Here she was on a parallel with Megan. What a powerful signal! To put it in another, more technical way, she had identified with her daughter. The adult Deborah had stepped aside for the little Debby, under the impact of an emotional recall she was only dimly aware of. Talking it over with a friend and seeing the differences between herself and her child, she could re-affirm the adult aspect of herself.

How did this help Deborah in her adult life? First, it was a good start to learn how to not get the two of them confused again. This helped in future situations where the pull of another parallel event, a replay effect, might recur and let her slip again. Second, it confirmed her sense of competence as a mother and pride in her daughter.

Being the parent of a school-aged child means having to speak with teachers, principals, school nurses and others. For those of us intimidated by authority figures, this may be difficult, even for the assertive among us. Like Deborah, we may find it hard to know when it is reasonable to intervene and when it is better not to.

If we keep in mind that our child has a temperament and constitution all its own, we can avoid trying to mold it into a set image (as well as typecasting ourselves!). Sooner or later some of these children's doings or sayings will really surprise us. This surprise itself, if not stifled, can become an important catalyst for our change. We have already seen some of these surprise effects in earlier chapters (see also Chapter One, p. 17). Here follows another:

Rachel had a discussion with her seven-year-old daughter's elementary school teacher. The teacher explained that Melissa could not wait her turn in class, often speaking out when others were still answering. Repeated explanations that "everyone gets a chance to answer," even disciplinary action, had failed to curb Melissa's habit of interrupting. Rachel was shocked. As a girl, she had suffered from an impatient mother who would not let her finish her sentences and joked about her being able to read Rachel's thoughts. Now, here was Melissa, two generations later, displaying her grandmother's habit! Since grandmother lived far away, Melissa had probably not picked it up from her. "Did I somehow pass on to Melissa what I found so disturbing in my own mother?" Rachel had to ask herself. She knew that it was not uncommon for grandchildren to mimic traits of their grandparents. Is it an inherited pattern? Do parents replicate these traits unaware, passing them on to their kids? With all these doubts, Rachel gingerly approached the topic of Melissa's behavior in school. The little girl looked at her and said calmly, "Well, you do that too!"

Rachel was indignant. She was sure not to behave that way, certainly not with Melissa. But she also knew how she had cultivated her daughter's candor and she did not want to penalize her for it now. So she asked for an example. It came right away: "You never let Mrs. Crane finish what she is telling you. You think she is dumb."

Rachel was flabbergasted. Melissa was right! Whenever she and Melissa met this elderly lady in the elevator, she felt roped in by Mrs. Crane's need to chat. Rachel winced, thinking of her peremptory treatment of their neighbor. She only wanted to get on with what she was doing, but had given her daughter a lesson in rudeness. Now she had to explain that even grownups can forget to treat others with respect when they are in a hurry. "Even your Mommy has a hard time with it, as you have noticed." She concluded with asking if Melissa could think of similar times herself, at school perhaps?

The daughter's observation had surprised the mother into a realization she had missed so far. As she pondered it, Rachel could remember other instances of abruptness her husband would point out to her, only to get her annoyed. It was not a pleasant or easy discovery to make. However, she was able to listen to her child's criticism and see a part of her mother in herself; a part she needed to tone down. Over time, with more of these sequences, Rachel learned to do just that.

This vignette brings out an aspect of sequences we are already familiar with but have not yet given its due. It is the open criticism from our own children. This makes many of us uneasy.

Since sequences are important child-effects for us, and we wouldn't want to miss them, perhaps we do well to take a look at this potential stumbling block to see how some of us have dealt with it.

Let's face it, we find it hard to accept critical comments, especially when they are justified. When our own flesh and blood seems to turn on us, it takes real fortitude to keep our cool. Or does it? Apparently, this is an old problem. A 17th century French commentator recorded: "There are no visible vices or physical blemishes that are not spotted by children; they observe them immediately and they know how to talk about them in acceptable language. One couldn't be more felicitous. Once grown up, they are burdened by all the imperfections they once derided on their turn".[xxix] Come to think of it, it has often struck me how both accurate and unemotional, sometimes even loving, these kinds of comments from our children can be. Some we have already heard and more will come.

We parents can learn to take our children's comments in stride, whether said in love or anger, inflated by passion, or whispered against shame or fear. The essence of this book is that we hear what they have to say, pay attention to the truth in it, and think carefully on our response. We need this feedback on our behavior. No other source has quite its candor, directness, and emotional impact. If we stifle it, we loose an impetus for doing better, which is a parental benefit.

A rather obvious example of how children's comments are needed for parental development is what happens in immigrant families. Unless the parents isolate themselves in an ethnic enclave, their children will assume a needed function for these new Americans. Once they work or get out, their social and cultural habits will be challenged. They need to learn a different social behavior. What their kids bring home from the classroom, playground, or street, needs to be integrated with their old traditions and efforts to adapt. "You don't have to wear a coat every time, Mom." "People don't say that here, Dad." "Ricky's parents don't burp after a meal." The kids grow up among the natives and bring cultural differences to the baffled parents whose peers may be too polite or indifferent to point it out. The children's unselfconscious adaptation to the new world is passed on to their parents as a lasting contribution to their evolving identities as new Americans.

In this kind of child-effect, be it a symbol or a sequence, we recognize the form of "becoming a pupil" which we have seen before. The parent easily learns from the child. The more we love the teacher, the better we learn the lesson.

Besides straightforward education, as we saw above, such a situation can also yield a more personal gain for parents.

Juliette, whom we met when her toddler stumbled in Chapter Four, was in such a predicament. Again, daughter Rhonda helped her deal with it.

Rhonda is in grade school. Some mothers had been asked to come in to cook a dish the kids could help prepare and eat for lunch. Juliette chose her children's favorite: tomato soup with tiny meatballs. Little did she realize that this use of meatballs gave away her ethnic background, but it would be a novelty for Rhonda's class.

Juliette could remember feeling painfully embarrassed by her parents for something unusual that they would do. Juliette was determined never to embarrass her daughter in front of her friends.

Making the meatballs in the classroom, she realized her dreadful faux pas and wanted to crawl under the carpet. A throng of curious kids mobbed around her asking where the spaghetti was. When she finally dared to glance at Rhonda, she saw her happily at work on her finger-paint project with a friend, not in the least perturbed by her mother's outlandish cuisine. The kids had fun rolling the tiny balls and dropping them in the steaming soup. When lunchtime came, they all slurped down the new delicacy and told their parents about it when they were picked up. Alone with Rhonda, Juliette asked how she thought it went. "They loved making the meatballs like we do at home! Only Andy did not eat the soup—he never eats soup."

"Did they think it was funny to put meatballs in soup?

"Maybe, but they liked it. Do you like my painting, Mom?"

Still not convinced, Juliette popped the central question: "Did I embarrass you, Rhonda?" Surprise and silence followed. "No, Mom! I know you make different things. You are different."

It was not: "we are different," nor: "yes, a little bit, and why can't you be like other moms?" It was: "no, and I can see the difference and I don't mind. You did your cooking and I did my painting. We all liked what we did."

"You know," she told me afterwards, "when I saw her sitting there all by herself and having a good time while I was doing my thing with the meatballs, she would look at me once in a while and smile. There was nothing there of self-consciousness or embarrassment. She knew I liked making them. She loved them and her classmates' unfamiliarity only confirmed what she already knew: that her Mommy is different and that she accepts that. When I compare that with how I felt each time my mother stepped out of line! I decided to take a page out of Rhonda's book. She has enough confidence in herself already. Maybe I could do that too."

This exchange, and others like it, gave Juliette another chance to review and loosen some leftover identifications with her mother's ability to embarrass. She gained confidence based on her achievement. By becoming deliberately more like her daughter in this regard, Juliette became less like her mother. We see how the "replay-effect" in this sequence allowed Juliette to move on in her life with a little less baggage.

As our school-going kids are busy meeting Erikson's tasks of "industry" and learning the "technology of the tribe," we as adults find ourselves in the middle of our most industrious years. We are over our ears in the same technology; ascending the peak of our careers. We, as they, are busy learning and working, and conflicts seem, for the moment, in abeyance. We have established our families and social life begins to knock on our door again. The needs of our children shift, and we begin to think of finding a new balance between family and work. We are less tied down by the unending caring and feeding routines of babies, or the almost constant supervision of the preschooler. We are tempted with more free time. We have more work and money and more time for our own lives!

Hold it, please. These are prime years to be with our kids. We get our last chance to balance the influence from school and peers with our own. We can read to them, work and play together, while we reap the rewards of parenthood. Adolescence is lying in wait, as is our own mid-life medley. When the temptation to return to career or "our own life" gets too strong, we can expect our kids to call it to our attention. If we are tuned in to them, they will bring us back from that brink.

This happened to a college president:

"Shortly after she became president of Radcliffe, Matina Horner found herself dashing about the house one evening, changing clothes and saying goodnight to her husband and children before she left to make yet another campus speech. As she was going out the door, one of her sons stopped her with a quiet plea: "It's not like you're my Mommy anymore."

"It was then, with those big brown eyes flashing up at me, that I realized that raising those three kids really meant a lot to me," she says. "I decided that when I couldn't get home until late at night, I was going to wake them up if I had to, to talk with them. The rest of my family thought I was nuts, but it worked. When the children had something to say, they woke up and were ready to talk. And when nothing much was on their minds, we'd have a hug instead. I think you find ways to maintain the relationships you want to maintain," she adds, breaking out an incandescent grin, "but they're not the ordinary ways."

Even though it happened years ago, Matina Horner still values that incident as a poignant turning point in her approach to her family and career responsibilities.[xxx]

Sometimes the child does not initiate a sequence as directly as Ms. Horner's son did. But when we are attuned, a symbol can also speak loudly to us:

Phil, whom we met in Chapter One, had increasingly more work as his reputation as a reliable mechanic spread. Eve, now eight years old, was going to her first summer day camp. After the first day she came home listless and announced that she did not like it. "I have to do all the work; nobody helps me and I'm all by myself." Phil could hear a sense of isolation and being left out in her complaint. He realized that he had, during the preceding months, spent most of his free time with the younger son while Eve was in art class. He had hardly spent any time with her and it nagged him. When he asked her if that was what bothered her, she tearfully agreed and climbed on the couch to sit next to him. Like the college president, Phil made changes in his schedule and activities to devote more time to his daughter, and feel a whole lot better about himself as well.

Do we need a Ph.D. in psychology to translate a symbol? No. What we need is a listening heart, a keen ability to read between the lines, and an awareness of our own feelings and those of our child. Both the college president and the mechanic adapted their routines to the needs of their children. This kind of flexibility comes in handy when we have to navigate the shoals of our children's adolescence as well as the undercurrents of the middle period of our lives.

Outside Activities

During the school years, children begin to take part in a wide range of activities, from music lessons to sports to Girl Scouts, which bring them outside the world of their home. These activities open up a new world of friends, public performance or competition, with all the attendant feelings of connection or isolation, glory or shame.

It surprises us how deeply we can become involved in our children's activities, as if much more than enrichment were at stake. The kid can be a rebel or a conformist, class president or odd-man-out, but many of us seem to get sucked right into it with a passion the activity alone hardly accounts for. Where's that fire coming from?

We have heard of the "stage mother" or the father who is more interested in his child's Little League game than the kid is. Do these parents find it hard to look inside themselves? Is it possible that they would find there an old hurt or a shame never outlived, from an embarrassing moment or a recital that flopped? A "loosing it" that now has to be made up by proxy, as it were? If that is the case, the outside activities of their kids can become for these parents a second chance not to be missed. This time, darn it, you'd better do your (my) best!

Woe the unhappy child who fails to save the parent's bruised childhood self! We see the emotions emerge: tears, anger, guilt, embarrassment, resentment. If, however, we can listen to what the child says or watch what it does, we get a new insight that beats having to use our kid as a proxy.

When Kim's daughter, Stacey, was in fourth grade, she was asked to captain a volleyball team. Kim was surprised that Stacey seemed thrilled about being chosen. She was not very athletic or competitive, and tended to leave leadership to others. Kim, herself still a shy person, had painful memories of not being chosen for teams and avoiding challenges. Though she had outgrown most of it, she feared that Stacey could one day follow in her footsteps. The first weeks Stacey reported her team was winning. She was elated. Then her team started to loose. Kim quizzed Stacey about her management. Where did she put the best players? Was she keeping score properly? Did she get distracted? Stacey reassured her mother that she did everything right. On the day of the last game Kim waited anxiously, asking Stacey quasi-casually what the final score had been. "Well," said Stacey, smiling, "it was a great game and really close. We came in second." Kim wanted to know the score. "The other two teams tied with twelve, we came in second, with eleven."

"You mean, you lost?" Kim couldn't hide her disappointment.

"I guess so," her daughter said. "But really we came in second. Is there any more salad?"

"Oh...yes...I'm glad you had fun." Kim managed to say automatically. She couldn't believe Stacey wasn't devastated. On the phone with her mother the next day, Kim mentioned how annoyed she had been at Stacey's reaction. "Can you imagine? She tried to pretend that losing was really coming in second!"

Then her mother said, "It makes a lot of sense to me. It takes the sting out of losing. Since the other teams were tied, her team did come in second. The main thing for her was that she enjoyed the game and was proud of herself." Kim pondered her mother's point and had to agree. Winning wasn't the whole point. As a child, Kim had seen loosing as an indelible stain. This had set her up for disappointment and shame many times. By putting herself in Stacey's shoes, she could ease some of that pain. Kim began to embrace a less crushing self-appraisal. She could also start to let go of some of her pressure on Stacey.

Here was a mother who feared her daughter wasn't doing well enough. Her daughter's sequence provided her with an insight she needed to overcome an ingrained fear. It also pointed the way for her to evaluate her own performance in a different light. If she could remember this, she might avoid some of her severe self-criticism during the upcoming mid-life review.

The opposite can happen as well. Strange as it may seem, we can be threatened by the success of our children—if we see them as competing with us.

Leo, Greg's father, was, even at forty-seven, a "man's man"—tough, more than a little macho, still good at his golf game and full of stories of his earlier glories as an athlete. He had been overjoyed when Greg was born. There were cigars and drinks all around at the Legion post. He had left the care of the baby in his wife Lucy's hands, until he could take the kid to the ball games. But when Greg started to be interested in his brushes (Leo was a contractor) he was told not to mess himself up. When he did not yet dare to ride his bike without training wheels, Leo cajoled him and pushed him off…and had to run home for a fist-full of Band-Aids. "You'll never ride a bike if you can't take a fall", he muttered. When Greg joined the Little League, somewhat reluctantly, Leo was there often, reviewing his every move after the game. The better Greg got at it, the more faults his father seemed to find, and the less he came. But Greg did well enough on the team and the coach was talking about getting onto the high school team as well. Leo was equivocal. "We'll see," he said with a grin, "then he has to play with the big guys". From then on it went downhill.

That summer Leo was going to prepare Greg for his promotion. But he was either too busy, or it rained, and when they did practice and Greg didn't do things right, his father would grab the bat and ball, and return it to Greg reluctantly, often with a final comment like:" With your kind of coordination you'll never make that team."

After a few of these sessions Greg blurted out: "But Dad, you don't let me try. And if I do, all you say is how bad I am at it. You always do that and I hate it!"

Lucy got wind of the fiasco. She tried to reason with her husband. "If you discourage him, how do you think he'll ever do his best? Why don't you get off his case for a while?" Leo had heard Greg. He had become upset and angry, feeling the boy was ungrateful. "Look at all I tried to do with him! What do I get?"

Lucy calmed him down. "It may just be the way you go about it."

Leo had no reply. Of course he wanted his son to be a champ too, but he could not deny that he had gotten annoyed each time he had tried to help.

That was as far as he could go. Even with Greg's comment and his wife's help, he could see no connection between Greg's achievement and his own half-hearted response to it. It did neither him, nor Greg, any good. The best he could do was, sadly, to withdraw from the field and try to stay at the sidelines while Greg developed activities that were outside of his father's range, and found his own supportive mentors.

There was no sequence here. This father responded to the message that he was doing something that undermined his intention, and he responded as best he could. He could not get himself to realize how he had made their play or practice a matter of competition, one he always had to win, to shore up his sagging prowess. That same need prevented him from engaging in a sequence, which might have led to some collaboration. Sometimes we just run up against our own and very real limitations. We want to know where they are and pull back from what we are doing, if only to do no more harm, and trust that our good intentions will be appreciated.

SOCIALIZATION

The other period of play and learning where children and parents can develop hand in hand is socialization. This, of course, overlaps with the schools' unofficial curriculum. Learning how to get along with peers and make friends teaches us important lessons besides social skills alone.

During this period we collect experience with early friendships which ultimately flows into our love relationships. Here we begin to feel the comfort of loyalty; the pain of betrayal; the need for tolerance and being sensitive to the other; and the joy of mutuality. Some of these early lessons we can remember. If we can't, our kids sooner or later will remind us—as we shall see. Some lessons were never fully learned: the sorrow of a friend lost; the envy of another's achievement; the urge to be part of the "in-group." As Bettelheim observed: when these experiences recur, we get a second chance to come closer to a resolution. Here is an example:

Bill, a social worker, told me that his thirteen-year-old daughter remarked to him that he lets waiters and store clerks take advantage of him. She said it in a sympathetic way, so he decided to take it to heart and forgot all about it. Several weeks after his daughter's remark, Bill Jr., ten years old, complained that his classmates were bullying him in the playground. This was particularly painful to Bill as memories of his own schoolyard humiliations remained vivid and he still had difficulty asserting himself. His own father had died when he was young, leaving his mother, a meek but devoted woman, responsible for his upbringing. Bill Sr.'s wife had encouraged him often to be more outspoken. From his son's teacher he learned that Bill Jr.'s peers picked on him for not sticking up for himself. She intervened whenever she could, but—she raised her palms in the air—what could she do?

Bill recognized his mild-mannered demeanor probably was not the best role model for his kids. Bill Jr. would have to learn how to assert himself. Together they enrolled in a recreational judo class. After their judo classes, they would have a snack and talk about their fears of getting hurt or hurting someone else, the thrill of beating an opponent, and the growing confidence they felt. That summer, he enticed his son to go to summer camp. The vigorous sports, and the playfully aggressive father-and-son judo lessons, provided Bill Jr. with alternate role models. Bill Jr. began to stand up against the bullies and gained their respect. Bill Sr.'s colleagues were grateful when he confronted a notoriously intimidating chief and had him back down from a plan to demand "volunteer" work for a private project.

This example of a sequence in collaboration also makes clear that, where others have failed to move us, a child can. To change is hard. It requires sustained effort and clear motivation. Spouses or friends may have axes to grind, but "children, unlike adults, have no need to deceive themselves."[xxxi] Our ambition to be good parents gives us the oh-so-needed kick in the butt to get off dead center.

Louise is a woman whose otherwise happy life is marred by a tendency to be too sensitive to perceived slights and setbacks. She had been the only child of doting parents for eight years before her only brother was adopted. Though she was in school most of the time, he remained for her the usurper of her mother. Her father, to make matters worse, took a strong liking to the boy. As Louise grew older, any situation involving an element of rivalry or competition caused her pain. Occasionally this led to unpleasantness. An angry, accusing or tearful Louise had broken off some relationships she had cultivated. Her worst fears came true, but by her own hands. Louise became a mother of a little boy. As he grew up, she could not help but notice how well he coped with the everyday frustrations similar to the ones that still fazed her. "Wasn't Tommy supposed to come and play with you today?"

"No. He went to Eddy's party." Pause.

"But, weren't you invited to Eddy's party?"

"No."

"But…I thought Tommy never does anything without you."

"Eddy is his friend, too." Pause again.

"Aren't you a little upset?"

"No. Tommy is still my friend.

For Louise, a friendship would have been in jeopardy if she'd found herself in her son's position. When a friend forgot her birthday or was late with an invitation, she had learned to cover her pain with a smile.

That day Louise faced the dilemma squarely. She asked her son point blank why he did not feel hurt (as she would have). She was all set to identify with the pain she thought he surely felt, but he didn't. This voice from her own flesh and blood let her also identify with the equanimity he possessed, but she didn't. "It's all right, Mom. I have other friends, too. I don't have to be with Tommy all the time. He'll tell me about the party and we'll both laugh!"

When Louise told me about this incident, she saw not only how her son could already share better than she did, but that he could distinguish between getting attention, time, companionship etc. from a person, and being loved by that person. It was the crucial difference between being a friend and having one that Louise would always slip over, like over a banana peel.

This one incident did not transform her life with instant magic, but she kept thinking of it each time she saw her son's ease with this kind of thing. Whenever little frustrations recurred, she learned to smile at herself: "There I go again!" Over time, with countless repetitions, she gradually calmed and soothed this little imp inside her. She gave herself the kind of confident reassurance that came natural to her own child. She was more at ease with her friends and they with her. The whole process reminded her of a little tugboat nudging along the massive ocean liner and just with a little push at the right spot, changing its course. With the time coming soon that her life would revolve less around her son and more around her friends, having learned this could be a welcome asset.

It helped this mother to see these events as minor frustrations and tolerate them as such. Part of the social fabric is woven of tolerance for criticism. The next mother's experience shows that children can help us learn this skill as well.

Olga was a woman who grew up with a mother she remembered as being critical of her and expecting her to do the worst. Later in life she was made defensive by criticism from anyone, and heard it where it wasn't even intended. She had some difficulties along these lines with friends and associates, and later with her husband and children. Though she had benefited by psychotherapy, she mentioned that it was the frequent interactions and confrontations with her child, not the sometimes irritated explanations of her husband, that provided her with the needed forum to put her insights into practice and to begin to undo her defensive habit. "I'd watch them with each other and with me, coming home from school or practice, and hear how they kidded and cajoled, commenting or even criticizing each other freely, and how they took it if they had it coming. Boy! What a difference! I just watched them, almost hearing myself saying something quite different, and then listening how they handled it. It made me embarrassed at times, but I learned from them. I knew all along I had to do it differently, less defensively, but with them in mind I could actually begin to do it, and it worked!

"I remember when one of them came home with her sandwiches still in her lunchbox. She put them on the counter and said: 'Great sandwiches, Mom! Everybody wanted them so I kept them myself.' (I had absentmindedly put catsup instead of jam on the peanut butter. My husband likes them that way.) 'Just kidding, Mom,' she added, mixing herself a bowl of cereal. My irritation and shame melted. I just hugged her and said 'I goofed.' We laughed. 'Just kidding' has now become a way of packaging criticism around the house for me."

Olga had worked on understanding how her mother's criticism had made her feel about herself, and how she had to protect herself. Partly she became like her critical mother, critical now of herself. Partly she learned to sniff criticism a mile away and overreact to it. Her children gave her a chance to try out her hard won self-understanding on an almost daily basis, so she could slowly become less defensive and even practice humor now and then. We can say that with her kids she had another chance of growing out of her old patterns and learning a few new ones of her own.

Social skills are more than society's "rules of engagement." They include also the ability to act and respond adequately to one's emotions. Someone who keeps the stirrings of the heart all too private or ignores the sentiments of others, may end up being considered a "cold fish" or an "insensitive jerk." If we overreact emotionally, we mystify others who wonder what our real feelings are, and who may end up considering us hysterical or superficial. It is a real asset to learn how to play and respond to the strings and trumpets of the human orchestra.

Are sons and fathers more in need of this kind of learning than mothers and daughters? The latter seem to have a cultural permit to share their emotional life. For many an American male parent, affection or emotional intimacy with their sons seems taboo. *Sons on Fathers* is an anthology of writings from diverse American authors about their connection with their fathers. It makes for sad reading indeed. The editor, Ralph Keyes, writes: "When men gather to discuss common concerns, they return insistently to the emotional abyss which so many feel separates them from their male parents. When I looked at my relationship with my father, I mostly saw a void." Yet even here the influence of the child had a redeeming effect. The editor describes how he primed his father: "...In letters I told him that I wanted to get to know him better." The father responded by showering the son with his life's stories. This led to a coming-together of the two men, at first awkward, but later more easygoing.[xxxii]

Let's look in more detail at how a son helped his father loosen up emotionally, and how the father could drop some of his "machismo" thanks to his son.

Frank took his eight-year-old son, Peter, to see *Bambi*. Frank remembered seeing it as a child and wanted to share it with his son. To his surprise, Peter was restless and seemed bored. As they left the theatre, Peter said, "What a stupid movie. It was really dumb. Did you really like it, Dad?" Frank was puzzled. Were the current electronic superheroes eclipsing Bambi? He decided to discuss it further another time. Peter's disdain for sentimentality had sounded a little too forceful to be convincing.

At the next day's breakfast he told Peter, "When my Mom

took me to *Bambi*, I loved it. But when I saw it yesterday, I noticed how sad it really was. Didn't you think so?"

Peter shrugged, looking away, "No."

"Didn't it make you feel like crying when Bambi's mother died? That forest fire scared me when I was little," Frank added.

"Really, Dad? I am not afraid of fires. And I don't cry at movies. They aren't real—just a movie." Frank thought he had found what bothered his son: he had been sad and scared, but too embarrassed to cry. He said: "It's OK to cry at movies, Peter. Sometimes it even feels good. You don't have to be ashamed of it."

"Well, I didn't see you cry. You never cry. Guys just don't cry," Peter answered, looking at him. There it was! Frank bit his lip. It was painfully true. Did Peter know he had trained himself not to cry at movies? Even as an adult, he hated "tearjerkers" like *ET*. In college, he had kept his eyes dry when everyone in the theater cried at the death of a character in *Love Story*. He had to backpedal now. So he explained to Peter that even he, as a grownup, had a hard time crying; Peter could do so freely. Peter did not seem to be convinced. A few days later he snuggled into his parents' bed in the morning and told them his dream of that night. He was on a big sea-going ship with his parents and a lot of strangers. Suddenly there was a loud bang and the ship started to sink. He was drenched; his father was also wet and seemed to disappear. He jumped overboard into a lifeboat and woke up.

After checking if Peter had wet the bed, Frank and his wife fussed with the dream's meaning. Frank saw similarities with *Bambi*: a beautiful setting, a disaster, and then a loss. He thought the death of Bambi's mother had made Peter fear the loss of his parents, being left with strangers, or his father drowning in a sea of tears.

That night Frank talked some more with Peter. He asked gently, "Petie boy, were you worried that if you started crying at the movie you couldn't stop?" No response. "Or was it seeing

Bambi's mother die? Isn't that the scariest thing, thinking about your mommy dying?" Now Peter's eyes filled with tears. He nodded wordlessly. "I know, I know," Frank said quietly, wanting to hug his boy. "You hated that movie, it made you feel bad. I remember I felt like that too, when I was a kid." In uncovering his son's hidden fears, Frank now had to begin dealing with his own. He remembered all too well sitting in that dark movie house, realizing that even his parents could die. When he anxiously glanced over at his Mom, he saw her wiping away her tears! He had never seen an adult cry before. Now Frank was really horrified. Not only was his mother going to die, she wasn't even acting as a grownup!

The grownup Frank understood what his son was going through. He tried to reassure him. "You don't have to worry about us. Mom and Dad aren't going to die for a long time. If anything ever happened to us, you would not be left with strangers, but go to Uncle David and Aunt Judy and your cousins." Peter nodded, and his face cleared up.

Frank had learned at least two valuable lessons. He had pursued Peter's reasons for disliking the movie without dismissing, arguing, or judging Peter's opinion. He had found out that Peter's stiff upper lip covered feelings and fears, as did his. Frank had also uncovered some of his own, equally hidden, prejudice against expressing one's feelings. Where did his little boy's macho "guys just don't cry" come from? From who else than from his own Dad? "I have a hard time crying myself, but you can do it," sounded like: "Little boys can cry, big boys do not." Doesn't every little boy want to be like the big boys? Frank had to confront his arbitrary censorship over his emotional life and how he was hamstrung by it. This collaborative sequence starting with a real replay effect was a turning point for both males, son and father.

Another social skill has more to do with sharing and working cooperatively. We need it to get projects done together in which people depend on each other's contribution, and in which we discover that the whole is greater than the sum of its parts. We also need it in the coming stages of our lives, when we assume the care for others (generativity) and depend on others for our integrity. Team sports, of course, stimulate this cooperation powerfully. But for someone who, like the father we are going to read about, did not have these experiences in childhood, his children will inevitably in some way provide a belated chance to play catch-up.

George was a father of four children, all close in age from seven to fifteen. He took pride in being a good family man, spending time with all four in diverse combinations and activities. As they grew up, however, it just seemed hard to let them take over. "Can I hold the drill, Dad?"

"Not yet son. It's heavy and you might get hurt."

"Can I use your paint?"

"It's so hard to get out of your clothes, sweetheart. Mommy won't like it when you do. Aren't your crayons good enough?" he would say while tying a shoelace on her shoe. Gradually, they would just do things without his permission. He would find out about it and get upset. Then he'd have to retreat and think of substitutes for things that were really too risky for them to do.

"When will you let me chop wood? I know I can do it. You just want to do everything yourself and it's not fair," his oldest son would say.

His wife had noticed it. "Try to do things *with* them. Let them make mistakes. They will learn better that way than by watching you." He would agree and try, but soon enough, forget all about it. He was like a man who held on to a rope for too long and whose fingers have to be pried loose, one by one.

Then he got another nudge, this time from his thirteen-year-old daughter. One day, when he was atop a ladder closing some cracks in the cabin wall that might let some winter air in, she came and watched him for awhile. Then she remarked casually, "Whenever we go on vacation, Dad, you're always fixing things." Her tone was one of qualified admiration and George heard it. It hit home. She was not exactly critical, but was observing his drive. Down came George from his perch, shaking his head and vowing to make family vacations more leisurely.

Summer came with the long-awaited camping trip. George was up before anybody else, stowing the gear in the truck. "I'm already tired," he joked, pulling out of the driveway.

"We could have helped you, Dad," was his oldest son's sad commentary. The others chimed in, to their mother, "We wanted to help, but he wouldn't let us." He hadn't even heard their offer. As he drove, their words kept turning over in his mind: "We could have helped you." If he had let them… Darn! He blew it again. They had camped before. Why not let them? He grew pensive. What if something went wrong? Well, what if? Little things can be important when you camp! Are they *that* important? "We could have helped you, Dad…"

When time came to pitch camp, he feigned to check the carburetor. He busied himself. Without much fanfare, the youngsters set up camp, asking for advice only occasionally. George just watched. Tents went up and the fire was going, the skillet sputtering with bacon and potatoes. He needed to tighten only a few lines. It had worked! The next day he found out that his oldest son was actually better than he was at siting the tents; the next older at leveling the ground; the two youngest at making a roaring fire with carefully selected sticks and firewood—each doing his share in a relaxed way and having fun with it. He tended to do all things in a hurry at the same time, and somewhat sloppily. "I could have told you," said his wife when he confided his relief and sadness. "They had more fun too. I'm glad you can see it now."

George later looked back on this vacation as a turning point for him. He had become the senior advisor of a well-coordinated team instead of a managerial, let-me-do-this-for-you parent. He applied this experience to aspects of his work, too. He let go of his monopoly on responsibility. In return, he found the pleasure and satisfaction from seeing his kids' competence and self-reliance. What a difference it made for all!

The comments of George's children and his wife's coaxing had "softened him up" for this collaborative shift, which in turn initiated a more collaborative style in his family. His children felt free to give an occasional reminder, as they noticed him making some changes in his old Daddy-does-all pattern. George was now better prepared to join the larger community, which would inevitably happen after the kids left. His learning more about collaboration would be useful for any generative activities, such as mentoring.

Now we want to look briefly at two other developmental tasks for adults that emerge in this period: the adaptation to the three-generation family, and the future task of integrity. The first task ushers in the bittersweet reality of how to deal with the aging and dying of our parents. The second task, integrity, needs moral and spiritual growth to keep ourselves whole and together, facing the end of our own death. From each of these two tasks, I will give one example.

ADAPTATION TO THE THREE-GENERATION FAMILY

Driving home after Thanksgiving dinner, Henry and Lynn were drained. Their children, Abby and Sally, ages seven and nine, were singing in the backseat. Trying to ignore them, Lynn said wearily to Henry, "Well, at least we got through the week-end." For Lynn, visiting her parents for the holidays had become progressively harder as time went on. The kids had been boisterous and Lynn's parents' small apartment could barely contain them. The food was heavy and fattening. Lynn had told her mother not to overdo the cooking, but her mother had insisted, though she seemed overwhelmed and had to take an extra dose of her arthritis medicine. Her dad had talked about retirement and stories of neighbors she no longer knew.

Abby and Sally kept chanting: "Over the river and through the woods, to Grandmother's house we go," louder each time.

Lynn exploded. "I asked you girls to keep it down! Can't you see I'm trying to talk with Daddy? Now be quiet please."

The noise in the back seat subsided, crayons replacing chant. Abby said, "Look at my turkey! Wasn't Grandma's turkey yummy? I liked that best. And you?"

Sally replied, "I'm glad she made mashed potatoes and sweet potatoes with all those cherries and marshmallow in it"

"Yeah," agreed Abby, "and isn't their apartment cozy and cute?"

Lynn, eyes closed, half-listened to her girls. *Naturally*, she thought, *what I hated most is what they liked best. The sweet potato pie was dreadful.* She dozed on and tuned in to the quiet girls' talk in the back. Their voices were soothing. Like her mother's had been. They loved their grandparents. They had enjoyed the feast, but Lynn's tastes had changed. She knew she had once liked her mother's cooking and her household. She was beginning to warm up to her daughters enjoying it now. She couldn't bear to think of her parents as elderly, infirm or in pain, but they weren't invalids yet. She couldn't depend on her father's financial advice, nor on her mother's guidance, but she could still enjoy their company and the relationship between them and her children. Perhaps there was even something she could do for them.

First this mother had reacted to her children in a knee-jerk fashion, unable to share their feelings. But by turning to their conversation and musing on it, she had found the beginning of comfort and acceptance. She still had to deal with her parents' aging, but her discontent about the event was muted. Seeing the world through her children's eyes had offered her a much needed perspective, clearing the way for her to feel less irritated about the aging of her parents and more compassionate.

The three-generation family is like a kaleidoscope. It keeps presenting new patterns each time one of its components makes a move or a step along the developmental paths. We have already seen this in Chapter One, when the grandparents predicted disaster from the way Jane and Bob raised their grandchildren. We will come across some more in the following chapters. For now, we can try to look for examples in our own families and be aware of this chance for us to catch some of the spin-off rewards when our children, or our elders, take a step along their way and invite us to respond and fall in step with them. We can see through their eyes, as Lynn in the vignette we just read, and identify with them, or we can simply learn from their example or be inspired by them.

INTEGRITY AND MORAL DEVELOPMENT

The grade school years are often seen as our last chance to impress our values upon our kids. In this book we are less concerned with this than with the influence of children on parents. What about children setting in motion a moral or spiritual development in us, the grown-ups?

In his book *The Moral Intelligence of Children*, Robert Coles gives us a personal example.

"...I was driving my nine-year-old son to the hospital. He had injured himself in an accident. I raced and at one point I ignored a yellow light, then immediately a red light, at which point my son intervened. Amid the headlong rush he said: 'Dad, if we're not careful, we'll make more trouble on our way to getting out of trouble.' This is what our children can offer us, and what we can offer them, even as we try to teach them. On that speedy trip to the hospital, my son was helping shape my character…asking me to stop and think about right and wrong, good and bad. My son had become my moral instructor that day."[xxxiii]

This reciprocal instruction happens along the way of raising children, as we have also seen in Chapter Four, where a mostly honest Tim had to clarify his values for himself at the insistence of his daughter. This process can be more fundamental, even reaching into our religious commitments at the time our kids go to their Sunday school or Temple.

Consider what happened to the loggers of Laytonville, California.

This small lumbering community became disturbed when their second-graders came home, asking questions like: "Papa doesn't love trees any more, does he?" They had been reading Dr. Seuss' little book about the Lorax and the Truffula trees, a morality tale in which the trees were all axed to be made into sweaters, flattening the forest into a wasteland. The parents tried to pull the offending book from the school's reading list. Some weeks of heavy discussion and reading of Dr. Seuss' book followed. The school board voted to table the decision for some time.

We do not always appreciate the challenge of our own brood to our values. Shall we put the monthly paycheck before the forest? Do we give up smoking, or heavy drinking, when drug education classes set our kids to question our habits? What do we say about social justice when junior is indignant after watching a TV program on homelessness? The columnist who wrote about the Laytonville incident concluded: "When parents react to a child's prodding with alarm, it isn't just because the questions are troublesome, it's because we cannot form an answer that rings right in our own ears."[xxxiv] An answer may be hard, too hard. But an honest attempt to struggle with the question on our part, including the opinions of our children, will benefit their understanding of the complexity of the world and will further our moral development as adults.

A moving example is given in the life and career of Robert Coles, the child psychiatrist and author of many books on the life of children. Coles refers to a particular experience that helped shape his devotion to this study, and the consequences it had for his career and spiritual development. We take the following from an interview:

Asked what led to his work with children: "I witnessed the early struggles of children to get into desegregated schools. I drove by one of the schools that was desegregated. I saw hundreds of people massed in front of the school, screaming and shouting and threatening one little black child who went into the school all by herself. Here you had a little girl all alone in a school building with a mob telling her every day that they were going to kill her. I thought to myself, *Maybe if I get to know a girl like this little girl,* whose name was Ruby Bridges and who became a heroine and teacher of mine, *I would learn a lot from her and maybe I could be of some help to her and her family.* This began this work. Asked by the interviewer: "Was it Ruby who walked past the angry mob smiling, and when a white woman asked her, 'What are you smiling at?' she looked up and said she was smiling at God?"

Coles answered: "Yes, this is the girl. This is the girl whose religious and spiritual interest I heard and took note of."[xxxv]

Coles went on to publish his well-known series of books ("Children of Crisis") which won him the Pulitzer Prize. Around the encounter with this child and others, his career crystallized.

As in the other examples of child-effects we have already seen, one single encounter with a child rarely turns us around. For this to happen, we usually need a series of them, a sequence, as well as a readiness to be turned around.

The relaxed time for parenthood will be over soon. We have, like the parents and adults in this chapter, spent time with our kids and loved them. We have listened respectfully to what they said and carefully interpreted what they did. We have mulled it over, talked with a spouse or friend, and we have checked it out with our own experiences. We have reacted to them in a mindful way and we have learned. The more we love the teacher, the better we learn the lesson.

With these gains we have added to our maturity and can make the most of the next stage, when our youngster turns the corner of puberty and is caught up in the currents of adolescence, and we are ready for our own mid-life review.

CHAPTER SIX

THE TESTED PARENT:
ADOLESCENCE

Like its politicians and its wars,
society has the teenagers it deserves.
J.B. Priestly

One evening I received a telephone call from Beatrice, a former patient. A law school professor, Beatrice was the widowed mother of two children. Several years previously, I had treated her for depression following her husband's sudden death.

She called in a crisis. The previous day, her sixteen- year-old daughter, Christine, had made an error of judgment. She was babysitting, a job Beatrice thought she was responsible enough for, but Christine had forgotten to bring some books she needed for her homework. Beatrice was working late, so Christine couldn't ask her to drop them off. She noticed the keys to the couple's other car sitting on the mantelpiece. The baby was sleeping, so why not make the run back home for her books? She grabbed the keys and headed out the door. Everything went as planned, until the drive back. At an intersection, a driver rammed her from behind. One of her car's taillights was smashed. A delay followed while she exchanged information with the other driver. Fortunately, the baby was still asleep when she arrived back at the house.

When the couple returned, Christine told them what had happened. They accepted her apology, but said they would have to call her mother.

Beatrice called me the following evening.

"I'm really torn," she said. "Tomorrow I'm supposed to leave for a seminar in Virginia Beach. I'd planned to take Christine and stay a few extra days so the two of us could have some time together. Now I don't know what to do."

She told me that Christine was contrite. Should she cancel her trip and ground her, or what? The first years of her daughter's adolescence had been difficult, but they were just now turning the corner, then this came along. "I can't pretend she just made a simple mistake. Something truly dreadful could have happened!"

The conflict between taking a punitive, corrective role and groping for a different, caring response, was evident. To understand her distress and to appreciate how Beatrice came to deal with it, we need to go back to where she came from.

Beatrice had been raised in a troubled family. She and her younger brothers lived with their father. The mother left to pursue her social career and a number of husbands. Her father was stern and demanding; a compulsive worker who spent little time with his three kids. Her life became a nightmare. After the divorce, her father made Beatrice and a housekeeper responsible for her brothers' upbringing. If he disapproved of their appearance or how they were doing in school, it was Beatrice who heard about it. This premature responsibility for her brothers placed a burden on the young girl's shoulders. Caring for her brothers combined with fear of her father, soon swallowed up whatever claims she might have made for her own budding independence.

While in therapy, she described memories from this period. She had a stony conviction that she had to take care of everything, the sense that no grownup would take her predicament seriously. One price for her competent, efficient adolescence, was an adult difficulty in asking for help or accepting it when offered.

School was the one positive aspect of her life. Bright and conscientious, she became a star pupil. The same qualities caught the eye of a college professor, whom she married in her sophomore year. Finally someone who would care for her and share the responsibility with her.

For Beatrice and her husband, work was as important as love. Beatrice found in academic achievement some of the support and protection that she had craved as a child. With her daughter Christine, she had a somewhat tentative bond. Her husband's sudden death brought her closer to her daughter.

She worked as hard in therapy as she had in school. She pulled out of her depression, gaining some understanding about her vulnerability and strength. Although asking for help remained difficult, she dealt with it by staying in touch with me through notes. Over the years, Beatrice kept me posted on how she became more open and more available to her children. Later, she developed an attachment to an architect. Then came the call.

"What do I do? Cancel my trip? Go alone? I can't let this go by!"

Beatrice was in conflict between her desire for a caring bond with her daughter and the strict model of childrearing she'd absorbed from her father. By the time Beatrice called me with her dilemma, I had become attuned to the child-effects described in this book and was actively listening for them in my patients' stories.

I asked what her first impulse had been. "To throw the book at her! Teach her responsibility!"

Leaving aside what else this reflex might have taught Christine, I asked her if that exclamation sounded like someone she knew.

She was silent for a few seconds, then spoke. "I guess I sound like my father." She sighed. "I thought I'd moved away from all that."

How would she have liked him to react if she were in Christine's shoes and got along the way she and her daughter did?

She answered quickly. "To take me along and listen to me, and work something out."

This, of course, was something that her father had never done. She had wanted to be listened to and respected; recognized as a responsible partner in an exchange. Instead, he had talked down to her. Eventually Beatrice shut up, and shut him out. Now she wanted something better for herself and for Christine.

Beatrice still had some leftover work to do about her sense of helplessness and rage. She already had a better way of loving her daughter. She was open enough to benefit from what only her child could give—the affirmation that she was a competent parent.

By casting the situation in terms of what she would have wanted, she formulated her own course of action. She took Christine along, encouraged her to talk about what accounted for her uncharacteristic lapse of judgment, and asked how she wanted to make up for it. They actually had a good time together. She even had to tone down some of Christine's more severe proposals for restitution. At the end of their trip, walking along the beach, her daughter suddenly hugged her, saying, "Thanks for being such a good Mom! I'm sorry for what I did and it feels much better now." This was exactly the balm Beatrice needed. Beatrice had settled an old account, learned from it, and could move on. She had resisted the impulse to act as her father would have.

She took the tack she wished her father had taken with her. Had he taken a similar approach, he might have contributed to her sense of mastery and autonomy. Instead she was left filled with self-doubt and helplessness.

Beatrice eventually learned to recognize and trust her feelings. She became close to her children, devoting herself to them as her own mother had never done. She welcomed Christine's and her brother's emerging adulthood. She had even noticed how her children's comments had helped her along, encouraging her to try something new or giving her an insight.

Since the incident that prompted her call, Beatrice has begun to rely on her children's comments more often. As with so many parents who become aware of child-effects, she remarked one day how much richer and open her life had become on account of it. Now she could begin to temper her resentment about her parents with a sad acknowledgment that they had missed out on the contributions she and her brothers could have made to their lives if only they had been open to it.

A not unusual adolescent problem is how to handle the new responsibility, and for their parents it is how to deal with their inevitable trials and errors. As with Beatrice, we get one more chance to raise our child, now almost an adult, and rewards for ourselves in the process.

WHAT HAPPENS IN ADOLESCENCE

Adolescence is the grand finale of childhood. When childhood has gone well, adolescence is rarely a big surprise. In case you haven't listened closely enough to your child in the preceding stages, this stage is a "last call" to start the process.

If childhood is a series of rehearsals for adulthood, then adolescence is a dress rehearsal. After that, the directors can lean back, maybe make an occasional change or correction, and, as the show hits the road, wait for the reviews.

So it is with us parents when our children enter adolescence and we with them. Most of our child raising has now been done. The child will soon be on its own and may need only to be reminded of what has been learned and to review it, try some new approaches, or find out how far it can go. All the earlier developmental steps will be repeated, but now with the compelling force of hormones and an eager audience of peers. A sneak preview of adulthood is thrown in: sex and independence. A busy time is had by all.

As we already saw with Beatrice, there will be plenty of opportunity for us parents to revisit and review our own earlier selves and, with a little help of our experience with our children, make some changes and corrections in our own scenarios as well.

The media-stereotype of the out-of-control adolescent as a deeply troubled, confused and an acting-up terror, is fortunately just that. Stereotypes are hard to weed out. Surveys have shown that this caricature does not fit most youngsters from reasonably well-functioning families, where the parents have been tested by the experience and found to be "good enough."

Research over the years confirms that most adolescents function well, enjoy life, and are happy with themselves most of the time. They lack major problems with their body image, and sexuality is not a significant problem. Adolescents do not feel inferior to other persons and they do not believe that others treat them poorly. Teenagers are relaxed under normal circumstances and are confident in their ability to deal with most ordinary life situations, and with new and challenging situations as well. The crucial thing is to understand the individual adolescents as they grow up.[xxxvi]

In descriptions of adolescent behavior, the most noisy ones get the spotlight. The same is true for other media creations: politicians, or other public figures, good and bad. Hardly a cross section of the population.

If your adolescent is having a very hard time getting through this phase, and is acting as he or she never did before, you may not find as much help in this chapter as you would like. Such troubled teenagers can not only risk their own well being, but also that of their parents. You might be better off seeking help for your child and yourself from experienced people such as other tested parents, competent therapists or well-trained counselors.

MAJOR THEMES

Some of the major themes that were already introduced earlier in childhood will return during adolescence. They are the developmental goals that await yet another round of trial and practice before the person is more or less ready to assume his or her role on life's stage. One of these is the move away from parents to peers. What is needed to complete this move in good order is a healthy dose of autonomy, independence and responsibility. We saw an example of this already. Another theme is the harnessing of the surge in power (muscular, emotional, hormonal) for the purpose of enhancing life and community. We shall see an example of this in this chapter. A third theme is mature sexuality. This calls for more than the ability to achieve orgasm. The task that integrates all of them is also the prize for this stage of life: identity and our place and role on the stage of the world. "Me Tarzan, you Jane" is about the most elemental summary of it.

Let us now take a closer look at how some parents manage to benefit in their own growth from their children's passage through the ups and downs of adolescence. The plot thickens when we realize that many parents are by this time in their own mid-life transition. This could be called our "second adolescence," because it is also a period at the end of which we are compelled to take stock and come to terms with major changes in our bodies, our social expectations and identities. Careers, jobs and marriages are often restructured as a consequence of it. George Vaillant, who researched the long-term changes in (male) adult lives, concluded that: "middle-aged adolescents" are affected by their own adolescent children. "These fresh identifications act as catalysts for change within adult personalities and allow for further growth."[xxxvii] A good, but technical, overview of this process can be found in Helen Meyers' article.[xxxix]

INTEREST IN PEERS

At childhood's end, our children begin to be more oriented to their peers than to their parents. We as parents accepted them, mostly, for what they were, but will their peers? In the dress rehearsal period, we see our kids getting preoccupied more with how they appear to other kids than how they look to us, their parents. Image becomes important. Belonging to a group and popularity gives each generation of adolescents their own "dress code" and music. It signals a balance between merging with the new group and departure from their elders. It is one dramatic way to deal with the necessary separation.

The teenager's relationship with friends can be illuminating for the parent, too. Show me your friends and I'll tell you who you are. As an example we will take Paul and his daughter Amy. How Amy chose her friends made Paul look at how he selected his. It woke him up to his own social limitations, enabling him to amend them.

Paul's grandparents had been immigrants. His parents were aware that they were different from the people around them. They had been embarrassed by their old-world parents, their accents, and their "funny" dress. To fit into American society, these parents modeled themselves after their school friends to better themselves. According to them, the only people worth knowing were those who were well off or had good social standing. Paul was allowed to invite only certain friends to the house.

When Paul was in fifth grade, he became friends with boys from his baseball team. His parents demurred; they made it clear that these children were not likely to help Paul get ahead. He was wasting his time with them. Paul remained friends with them anyway. In high school however, he stopped seeing them.

Since this and other experiences, Paul has adopted his parents' attitude, as became clear when his daughter Amy made her friends. He had earlier vowed no to treat Amy as he had been treated, but he complained to his wife that he didn't care much for Amy's friends. He restrained himself. He did not criticize the friends to Amy directly. When Amy showed him the list of people to invite for her fourteenth birthday party, Paul asked: "Do you have to invite so many? Why not just two or three really close ones?"

"But who would I not invite?" Amy asked. Paul named several girls he thought Amy could do without. "But I like those girls," Amy said. "And it would hurt their feelings not to be invited."

"Why do you like them, anyway?" Paul wanted to know.

Amy gave it some thought and said, "Sarah likes dogs; Molly always makes us laugh; and Kathy has such a great imagination." She looked at her father. "You don't really like them, do you?"

"Sure I do," he said, "I just want you to know how important it is to choose your friends carefully. Your friends can do a lot for you."

Amy was taken aback. She paused, and said, "I don't choose my friends like you do, Dad. I don't care if they can do something for me. I just like them."

That comment hit Paul like a ton of bricks. It was the kind of thing he wished he could have said to his parents instead of taking on their prejudice. Amy had unwittingly confronted him with his muted adoption of his parents' outlook, even while he knew it was a shallow one.

It was incidents like this that prompted him to take a hard look at his social life. What he saw was not pretty. To be honest, using people had become second nature to him, in business and in his personal life. He wondered how many good friends he had—people he just liked a lot. The thought crossed his mind that, come retirement, he would still have to make them. Not pleasant! He remembered his regrets about distancing himself from his high school buddies. A few days later he actually sat down and wrote a letter to one of them. Lo and behold, he was able to rekindle the old warmth between them. With time, his group of friends grew to include people whose presence he just enjoyed, whether they were assets to him or not.

Because he had remained perceptive, responsive and had dared to be honest with himself, Paul had not only learned from Amy, he had also made a serious effort at a mid-course correction. He became a more personable man and friend. The discussion they had on the subject of friends, Paul's observations of Amy with her friends and his own reflections, led him to complete one more aspect of his emancipation from his parents and undo a limitation in his character that dated from his own adolescence.

Amy had started a truly effective sequence in collaboration. As a result, Paul could revive his earlier, more natural affection for others. Now he could continue a further maturation of his relationships. For the first time in years, he was able to think without resentment about his parents' attitude regarding friendships, and could see what was hidden behind it: their need to bolster a fragile new identity; an escape from being seen as outsiders. He and Amy had paved the way for his future task of connecting to the wider world, of integrity.

Observing your children with their friends does not always bring on such self-examination, but the effect on the parent can still be beneficial, even without drama. You may find that an unusual appearance, such as green hair with a nose ring, can hide a perfectly reasonable human being, as one mother discovered when she took the time to get to know one of her daughter's friends. You may see that times have truly changed. This was the experience of a father whose son always talked about his friend, who turned out to have a different skin color. The father had acquaintances of his own from various ethnic groups, but always mentioned their race when talking to a third person. His son's lack of interest in that aspect was a step ahead of his own progressive veneer. He began to wonder if he mentioned race only to show how tolerant he was. He began to question his own sincerity and pay more attention to what his friends were as people.

As with Paul, aspects of your child's social life can become a catalyst for your own growth. In Ruth's case, it was her daughter's effortless taking of the same hurdle that had tripped Ruth up in her own adolescence. The hurdle was being dateless for the senior prom.

Ruth had been a wallflower and a brain in high school. She was considered an oddity, not going out until her first date in college. Her daughter, Jennifer, on the other hand, had a full social life, but somehow found herself without a date for the senior prom. Together with a few friends, who were also dateless, three girls and two boys, they decided to go together. At a thrift store they bought funky clothes, fifties-style, dresses Ruth could have worn had she gone to the prom. Jennifer's was yellow chiffon with spaghetti straps. Dressed to kill, they pooled their money and rented a limo to arrive at the prom in style.

Just watching this crisis unfold made Ruth remember how miserable she had been all through high school. Her oddball status had made her feel like a loser. After Jennifer sailed away to her prom, Ruth felt relieved, but also a little envious. She then realized she had carried this loser image with her for too many years. This self-image was not only completely out of date, it was cockeyed!

Ruth was happily married, had many good friends, and enjoyed her work as a computer programmer. Her old high school status had not mattered in her life in a real way. Thinking back on those years, she realized now that it was time to update that old image and the feelings that went with it. She needed to get on with her life and enjoy the party!

Jennifer's resourcefulness and spunk were just what this mother needed to nudge her over a threshold, to help her write a happy ending to an awkward chapter in her past, to take full possession of her present, and to move into the future. Jennifer had given her an unmistakable symbol. Ruth had paid attention to it and to the upsurge of feelings, and had worked on it. She had understood them. Whenever the old loser feelings would creep up, all she had to do now was to think back to Jennifer's prom and smile.

Throughout our children's adolescence, we have to build on the groundwork that we laid in all those years of childhood: shifting gradually from holding and controlling, to letting go; from guiding and advising to stepping aside and maybe raising questions or discussions as soon-to-be equals; from teaching and modeling values to handing over responsibility to our young adult. If we started this process early enough and if we kept its momentum over the years, both we and our adolescent children will be prepared for the dress rehearsal for adulthood. If we did not, then this stage is not the best time to catch up with this slow process of becoming a new individual. Much of adolescent grief can be traced to the insufficient preparation of the youngster and the parent. There simply were not enough rehearsals.

Wait! You will say. Adolescents aren't ready to take on the world! You are right, of course; they are not yet. But they are, by the same token, no longer children, and they will not hesitate to remind us of their new status. Things are possible for them that were out of reach before. A teenager may have a job outside the home, if only babysitting, to gain a new level of responsibility and independence. They can earn money, drive cars, go out on dates, and adolescents, having grown into adults (physically speaking that is), become sexually mature.

Sexual Maturity

The awareness that your child is now able, at least biologically, to have children of its own, can come as a shock, though hardly as a surprise.

Thus John was in for such a shock. On a beautiful summer day, he and the rest of the family helped his son, Rob, move from one college dorm to the next. Visiting Rob with Juliette, his wife, and their daughter, had always been an occasion to catch up, make plans, and settle details in the life of a college student. John enjoyed, and even seemed to need, these visits. He had been a very involved parent, participating fully in the children's early lives and raising them with Juliette. At times she caught him being the protective, guiding father too much, too long. Even Rob had begun to remind him that he didn't need it any more and would rather do without. It was hard for John to get off the Daddy-track!

But now they were all fully engaged in carrying Rob's belongings down the stairs, into the van, and up another cavernous hall. Rob had finished partying and packing in the hours before they arrived. His once so cozy room was dismantled; only some odds and ends remained.

"Something left for me to do?" John wanted to know.

"Not much Dad. Oh yeah, you could do the drawers," he said, struggling to disconnect his stereo.

John opened the top drawer. Assorted socks, some even in

pairs, keys, more socks, sunglasses, Chapstick, after-shave and…what was that? Trying to continue as if nothing had happened, he packed the socks, keys and the condoms in the carton. Slowly balancing the box downstairs gave John some time to recover. Robby, his son, had become a man! The little boy he had cuddled, carried on his back, played with, camped with, laughed and argued with, hugged and tucked in countless times, now had a life wholly his own, in which he played no part, of which he knew nothing. Of course he had dates, lately even intimations of a girlfriend, but didn't his studying and athletics take up most of his time? At least he was protecting himself—and her. Who was she? He started to muse. Did he feel left out? How old had he been when he bought his first condoms? Hey, was he getting a little jealous? Did he know what he was doing then? Did Rob know any more?

His preoccupation was not noticed in the noise of the move, nor at lunch in the cafeteria full of boisterous students and other parents. He could still feel the shock, but now it mixed with pride and even relief. His boy was all right. It was he, himself, who had a problem. Look at the strapping kid! What girl would not want him? No more kid to protect and play with. Grown now. A grown man-son, always his son, but more equal as time would go on; friends even, confiding, sharing, watching out for each other. He began to relax.

After lunch the family went for a walk by the river. The kids went ahead, chatting. He told Juliette about his discovery. "Well," she said, "Congratulations! At least he is careful." She had always been more matter-of-fact about life's vicissitudes than he could be. He then let her in on his early sense of distress, of loss even, and now of his pride and hope. She smiled at him. "You've done enough, Daddy. Sounds like both of you grew up a little."

This incident proved to be, for John, a critical signal of Rob's growing up and independence. John was able to get the message he needed. He let his boy be a man now, and let go of much of his protectiveness for a more mature concern about his well being. Had he made the wrong turn at this point, persisting in his old ways, he might well have become meddlesome, and Rob's irritation would have done their relationship no good. Less subtle signs of his independence would follow and eventually alienation might result. He would be stuck. Instead, John became his son's occasional advisor in moments of crisis and a trusted confidant. Prompted by his son, John had made the crucial step towards mature adulthood. No pain no gain.

John, and countless parents in this position, had to give up being the focus of their child's affections and see them turn to sources outside the home. How else do we grow out of being the temporary custodians; the trustees for that spark of life that was entrusted to us? This turning away of the teenager not only allows us to turn our attention again to our own lives with others, it also frees us to look forward to enjoying our child's company in a more mature way. We will be friends, but with a shared intimacy and history that forever reaches beyond other friendships. Lastly, it prepares us for the big bonus of parenthood: our joys as grandparents.

Becoming aware of your child's sexual maturation can entail other surprises; more than we can review here. We saw John discover his son's sexuality and confront his own need to maintain and protect his son's life as a boy. We now shall see how Carol saw her values being taken seriously, and how she came to terms with her need to compensate for her own parent's restrictions.

Carol and her daughter, Lisa, got along very well. Their relationship was honest and they listened to each other. Her ex-husband, Phillip, and her lover, Sharon, both acted as co-parents.

Carol's own upbringing had been conventional: a woman's place was in the home. Her ties with her parents got frayed when she divorced and took up with Sharon. Like so many aggrieved ex-children, Carol too, strove to do everything right that her parents had done wrong. She was going to let Lisa pursue her own goals!

Lisa was levelheaded and independent. A happy child, she started to go out with boys at fourteen, but Carol did not worry. Lisa was well prepared by their frank discussions and classes on sex education, she thought.

At sixteen, Lisa became pregnant, however. Carol was alarmed. Would she have to go through an abortion? Lisa would have none of it. She wanted the baby, not a marriage. She did not even expect help from its father. She would rely on her own family.

Carol lived in anxiety. How about finishing high school? What about the rest of her life? Carol had taken a long time to figure out what she wanted to do in her life, the training and kind of job she wanted. She had struggled hard to become the person she wanted to be. Was Lisa now limiting her choices too early? Carol also felt guilty. Had she made the untraditional role for women appear too difficult, or perhaps too easy? Could this be why Lisa got pregnant?

Sharon and Phillip stayed cool. In a four-way family conference, Lisa's plans were considered. She wanted to finish school. School had a day care center; she could nurse the baby between classes. Carol still worried. Would Lisa still have time for her friends, her photography, and her soccer team? Carol's job was time-consuming; she could contribute only so much to child care. Sharon and Phillip volunteered to baby-sit.

Finally Carol asked: "What about life after high school? This is your whole life we are talking about."

"You always said I should figure out what I wanted to do for myself," Lisa came back. "I'm not really sure yet about anything else, but I do know I want the baby."

This time it got through to Carol. She could begin to unhook her guilt and see her daughter as making her own choices. Lisa was really different from her. It was going to be *her* life, from now on.

"She made me put my money where my mouth was," Carol said later. "It got easier once she had the baby and I knew both were going to be okay. The baby is a sweetheart, even when he screams. Lisa makes time for her friends and her photography. I had wanted her life to be easier than mine. Well, in some ways it is. Being an unwed mother carries fewer stigmas these days. Lisa made me aware of my fantasy for her: a life without struggle and major hassles like I had. No bad rap for her. I wanted her to choose for herself, but face none of the hard consequences at the same time. Impossible. Even I like my life. It was hard, but there was no other way to get where I am now." Like so many of us, Carol found it very difficult to drop the role of protector for her child, especially when sexuality is the context.

We can't forever protect our children the way we could as long as they were small. We can't forever hold their hand when they take risky steps. They move into life with all their gifts and limitations, joys and tragedies.

Adolescence is a threshold to be crossed by parent and child together. The child moves into young adulthood. The parent moves into mature, late parenting, and the stage of the childless parent. Both assume their own lives. Adult development for both generations, the young and the old, can only proceed when the parent has transformed the love and link with the child into a new tie that no longer binds. If the parent can benefit from the child's influence, as John and Carol did, then this transition is eased for both.

We have seen examples of a few typical adolescent phenomena: the new responsibilities; the shift of the children away from the parents and toward peers; and emerging sexual maturity. In these instances, other major issues were implied also: the increasing independence and autonomy of the teenager and the establishment of an identity for the future young adult. Let us look at an example of this and see how a father benefited in his own adult growth, thanks to a spirit of willingness to be affected by a major change in his son.

Dick, a sophomore at a West Coast college, went to the Dean's office for help. His Dad had just threatened to withdraw financial support if "his boy" didn't come home right away. He was alarmed by Dick's involvement in the peace movement. Dad was a career military man living on a base in the Midwest. The time was the early seventies: campus demonstrations, drug busts, beards, beads, and draft card burnings. The country and families were split apart.

Dick tried to reason with his dad by phone. No success. Dad asked, "Are you on drugs, too?" With Mom in tow, he boarded a plane, ready to take (save?) his boy from the bad company he was ensnared by. Dick's one-way ticket was in his pocket.

Back at the school, in the dorm and Dean's office, plans for a reception had been made. Two friends accompanied Dick to the airport; clean-shaven, good-looking kids. The first stop after their arrival was Dick's room. No radicals there. No pungent aromas. Just books, athletic garb, and lecture notes. Next they went to the Dean's office. Looking out over manicured lawns, the affable dean chatted about how the school tried to educate its students not only in the arts and sciences, but for life, formulating what mattered most and why; helping them to learn how to make up their minds in an environment free from coercion. "Sometimes they come to conclusions that surprise their parents. That happened to me too, at that age. It takes some getting used to, doesn't it?" He smiled reassuringly. Mom and Dad were invited for lunch at the Faculty Club. By now the guests had become cautious and wrapped in thought.

A paneled room, oozing establishment and authority, was set aside for the gathering. Dick's advisor, his dorm tutor, and his roommates were invited. The conversation continued. Then Dad began to ask questions and listened to answers. Dick and his friends were respectful when they disagreed. The tutor praised Dick for his contributions to dorm life. His advisor mentioned his unblemished academic record. Both complimented the parents for having raised such a committed son; their sacrifices were not in vain. No one alluded to Dad's agenda. He and Mom sat through the animated lunch, slowly unwinding as the human factor gradually overcame whatever distortions had been fostered by distance and doubt.

They walked around campus. This was, after all, their first visit west! They saw the library, Dick's lab, even the cubicle where he did draft counseling. After spending the night in a hotel, Dad came back to the dorm the next morning, smiling. To the cheers of the roommates, he tore up Dick's ticket.

Some time later, Dick reflected on the change in his Dad. "He was surprised that the school supported me. He didn't know protest could be respectable. He liked the people he met. It was all very different from what he had seen on TV. It did not change his opinion on the war, but it did change our relationship. I used to be intimidated by him. We were never very close, but I liked him. I did not give in to him this time and he did not seem to mind as much as I thought he would. When I visited home last Thanksgiving, we got along better than ever. We respect each other now. We went hunting together; he with his gun and I with my camera."

This father, who feared loosing his son (this was adolescence after all), could very well have lost him had he stuck to his guns. Dick had not influenced him much as Dick grew up. Yet he managed, with a generous assist, to keep an open mind, and learn and listen to what his son and his new allies told him. He had come to accept his boy's emerging identity, which turned out to be liberating for them both. A potentially stark conflict turned into a growth-promoting event for father and son. Dick provided a sequence, which provoked Dad to reconsider and then drop his insistence on filial compliance. Now the two could continue their way amicably and not in opposition.

Where children are allowed from day one to affect their parents in the ways herein described, parents are less likely to see their children become like the cliché of adolescents as a captious, rebellious brood. Why don't they? Child-effects, especially symbols and sequences, imply that parents are willing to let their children have a say in becoming who they want to be. Not wanting to claim them as their own allows authentic growth. These parents encourage their children to assume responsibilities as their skills increase over the years. In such a family, authority and power do not become a source of conflict. These kids know it is gradually earned and acquired.

The example of Dick's father shows that even in families where this willingness is not abundant, the adolescent may yet work a significant change in the parent. In this process, the way to continue parental development is opened up. Dick's father was now freer to devote some of his energies to others that needed his generative impulses more than his grown son.

Seeing is believing. We believe that child-effects work when we see what happens to parents who, with the best of intentions, remain essentially deaf and blind to the words and actions by which their offspring comment on what the parents do to them. The parents we have met in this chapter, so far, were able to pick up on it and were rewarded in their own lives. Others are less fortunate.

I have met some of these parents in my life and I have seen some through the eyes of their children, who became my patients. Once I had become interested in how parents and children "raise each other," I noticed that some patients who took a longer than usual time to respond to psychotherapy had something in common. Between them and their parents, this give-and-take of influencing each other was minimal or absent. They both had gotten stuck.

The child (my later adult patient) had become accustomed to a relationship with a parent who showed little interest in what the child was trying to say or do, let alone in how the parent impacted on the child. From early on, such a parent remained focused on what it wanted the child to be. Trying to tell this parent that the shoes did not fit or that the child felt it was being misunderstood, fell on deaf ears. These children gave up trying and isolated themselves for protection. Some of them ended up believing they had little claim to a free, autonomous life. A standoff between parent and child ensued, with a painful and frozen relationship at best, and little room for either to grow.

Once in treatment, this painful standoff would be re-created, the patient feeling misunderstood and under threat, and I wondering why I felt so stymied and frustrated. It would take long and careful work for us to understand the history of this re-enactment.

Only then could they begin to believe that this time they were being heard, even assisted in growing their own way.

Dennis' parents will illustrate what can happen when child-effects are not welcome in the home.

Dennis' parents were hard working and honest. They grew their vegetables and raised their kids. Father was a contractor; Mother taught grade school. When they were home they were tired and quarreled often. Father always knew best; Mother deferred to him. Her personality was a little warmer, but she had a habit of going through the kids' drawers.

Dennis' older brother became a nuisance, with fights and scandals. At least he generated some late parent-child interactions. Dennis cowered in his shadow, vowing just to keep quiet. He withdrew, became resilient, often going on long, solitary walks. He remembers few good moments with his parents, nor any comfortable intimacy. His mother's interest in him while he bathed embarrassed him, but he did not protest. His best recollections are from summer camp.

He remembers feeling completely lost the summer before he went to college, spending days on end in a darkened room, eating little. His parents reacted with "get up and do something."

The parent-child relation was one-sided. When he became interested in collecting rocks or learning German, it was: "It's useless," or: "That will be too expensive." His silence, compliance, solitariness, even his depression during adolescence, did not provoke his parents to a true interest in his predicament or to an effort to get through to him.

At thirty-three, Dennis was not yet married. After four years with the Peace Corps in Malawi, he became program manager in a large company. He disliked his job, detested his superior and had contempt for his inability to get up and find another job. He described his life as "stagnation" and thought about suicide.

Therapy with Dennis went slower than usual. An important clue to what was blocking our progress was my feeling of being stalemated; checked by him. My comments or efforts were met with: "Doesn't that show how little you understand me?" and a caring gesture evoked anger for all I would not give him. I began to feel as he might have felt vis-a-vis his parents: insignificant, unappreciated, and powerless.

He almost had the tables turned on us so we would both lose. Almost, until I could show him that this stalemate had become his main protection against his parents and his world. But protection at what a price! Now we could shift to his effect on me. This empowered him. We could look at the result of his isolation. Mom and Dad had missed out on a joyous and proud parenthood and a possible relaxation of their own constricted styles. Dennis began to make progress.

At this point his mother still limited the conversation to current events. Physical expression of affection remained perfunctory. Father was accessible only through action, often negative; an argument, but rarely something constructive. Did he have feelings? Dennis wouldn't know.

Once, Dennis and his brother went back to attend a wedding. They noticed their parents sitting by themselves at a table. They overheard them saying to another guest that they couldn't understand why their own sons wouldn't even come to sit and chat with them.

This couple lived in a resigned, somewhat cold arrangement with little community ties. Their world had opened up a little when their children were born: car pools, PTA, Boy Scouts, etc., but few connections with couples in the same situation lasted. When the kids left home, no latent interest developed; no "late blooming" we so often see in middle age when the task of child-rearing is done.

Dennis' parents could not or would not pick up his signals, nor interpret his symbols, let alone take a part in a sequence he would start. They had lived together, but without each other. They should have been shaken up by his depression in adolescence. They had lacked the vitamins of their child's "otherness" to constantly challenge their way of life. Their growth was stunted; their late adult development was an example of stagnation and lack of integration. Dennis managed to get unstuck. His parents did not.

Valery presented an even more clear-cut sequence to her mother, Bernice. We can understand perhaps why this mother did pay no real attention to her daughter's input if we take into account that there was no tradition in this family of being receptive to child-effects.

Bernice was constantly criticized by her husband, who was a domestic tyrant and workaholic. Her job was to obey; to fit her life around his. Their daughter, Valery, was to be seen but not heard.

Bernice complained frequently about her joyless life with a husband who insisted that his life was more important than anyone else's. At times she threatened to leave him; once she actually did, but came back the same day.

Valery became a compliant child, obedient and quiet. She did not date in high school. "You are too young for such nonsense," her father decreed. She could hardly wait to leave home.

Nursing school was a breath of fresh air. Valery made friends and began to date. An affair with an older physician backfired and she fell apart when he left her. Without him she seemed to be nothing. She sank into a depression. Her work suffered. Despairing, with failing grades, she finally sought help from her priest-counselor.

With his help, she began to understand how her relationship with the doctor had mirrored her parent's arrangement; her mother's dependence on her father, whom she never challenged nor could leave. Valery saw how dependent she had allowed herself to become on the older man. She could even begin to feel her anger for letting him take advantage of her. Her energy returned, she did well in school again. On her rare visits home, she began to challenge her father's dominance, astonishing him, shocking her mother, and surprising herself.

Valery tried several times to talk to her mother about their lives. Instead of patiently listening to her mother's complaints, she encouraged her mother to seek help for herself, reminding her how it had helped her. At these points, Bernice got a chance to get engaged in a real conversation with her daughter, reviewing their lives, an exchange of experiences, and a self-examination. Valery offered her this possible sequence on a silver platter. Bernice did not grab it. She had also missed the earlier symbols of Valery's breakdown when her lover left her. She did not see her daughter's dependence on him as a copy of her own bond with her husband. If she had, Bernice could have begun to make some changes in her own life, instead of bemoaning her helplessness and ordeals. While Valery was going through life rather well, including even a somewhat more reasonable relationship with her father, Bernice remained locked in her impasse, which blocked her growth into a satisfying late adulthood.

We either grow together with our children or we don't grow much.

We have come to the end of adolescence for our child. "What end?" you may ask. "My kids are still at home, can't find a job, back from a bad marriage or back in graduate school." True, but is it the same home? Home may be where they can't refuse to let you in, and many young people have to return for a while. But they are nevertheless prepared enough to live in the outside world and make their contribution to it; they are young adults. Having raised each other, you too are now prepared to re-enter the world. The last child has flown the nest and you can begin to rearrange the furniture of your life.

If indeed child-effects have played a role, you have changed a lot since you put on that first diaper. By being a parent yourself, guiding (and being guided by) your children, you have come to a new appreciation and understanding of your own parents. Some old leftover problems from your own childhood have been put to rest. You have assumed a new and lasting identity and accepted a share of our responsibility for the world. You have your grown children as dear and close companions for life. You now care for each other, your community, and yourself, in an expanded, deeper way. Besides adding years, you have gained a different outlook on life and how it hangs together. From this vantage point, as one link in the long chain of generations, you may even get a glimpse of where you believe we are all heading.

We are now prepared for the next stage in our journey through adult development. The period Erikson characterized by the tasks of "generativity" and "integrity." Our caring shifts to others: the community, grandchildren, the future generations. One supreme task remains: to integrate a fairly coherent view of life, based on our experiences, history, and our concept of the future, which should keep the alienation and despair of old age at bay. For many of us, this growth involves also a deepening of whatever spiritual dimension we have found in life. The capacity to experience this dimension is yet another confirmation of the whole person.

A beautiful illustration of how this spiritual aspect can blossom in our "second adolescence" is given by Doris Lessing in her short story *The Temptation of Jack Orkny*.

Jack is a middle-aged journalist, a politically active man, whose father is dying. His children are on the cusp of young adulthood, in and out of the house. When Jack arrives at his dying father's bed, he meets his sister and brother. To their surprise, the dying man wants to see little of them, but keeps asking for one granddaughter, Ann. Ann finally arrives, and Granddad asks, "Who are these people? Who are all these tall people?"

Left alone with him, she sings an old church hymn. The grownups are taken aback again: "Yes, I'm afraid she is," they say to each other, "That's the bond, you see." That bond was formed earlier when Ann had visited the old man for Easter. The adults discussed religion, but at a distance. That night, Jack has the first of a series of unsettling dreams. His father died the next day while Ann crooned hymns, old tunes, and nursery rhymes to him.

Back home, Jack is confronted with the youth and activity of his son, the appeals from his political friends, and more dreams. Then begins Jack's stocktaking. He allows for new elements to be included: the love of his wife, his fears of death, his daughters' commitment to causes. They remind him of his own reality. He wants them to avoid his life's sad progression from idealism through action and disenchantment to cynicism. He gropes for "the desire to look at history, to absorb it, and in one bound, transcend it." A series of brief exchanges with his son, a political activist and atheist, and with his daughters, all three with their own brand of faith, keep his soul stirred.

The end of the story hints at the resolution of Jack's mid-life transition: "behind the face of the skeptical world was another, which no conscious decision of his could stop him exploring."

The roles of Ann and his own children as catalysts for his imminent conversion, are clear.[xxxix]

The rehearsal for your child's adulthood is now over. Like all dress rehearsals, it was a mix of brinkmanship and fun while the pieces began to fall in place. Your kids are on their own, equal players now and experienced collaborators. The curtain can rise for opening night.

Hold it! Wait a moment! Before we move to the next stage of adult life and the contribution children can make there, this may be the place to recall an earlier warning.

`The process by which parents allow themselves to be shaped by their children is not always so innocent. Due to its very nature, collaboration can be misused and lead to problems. Although this risk is present from the start, it is perhaps greatest in adolescence, when the child is more like an adult and more articulate, and the adult more vulnerable.

Once the collaborative mode of dealing with each other has been established in early parenthood, some parents may not want to wait for opportunities to arise, but may actively solicit the child for its opinions. Even before adolescence, they may want to know how they are doing as parents. They may ask their own children for advice on their social life or help in job decisions. What should be a voluntary give and take that respects the differences in responsibility and experience, can be perverted into a subtle form of child exploitation: "What should Mommy do?", "Should I take this job?", "Do you think I should date this lady again?"

When a parent becomes dependent on the child in this way, the natural roles between them are reversed. This role reversal puts a premature responsibility on the child; a weight too heavy for the child's shoulders. The child is seduced to become a super-kid, a premature adult, and is cheated out of a piece of childhood. It is easy to see how parents who become dependent on their children in this way warp the growth of the child and retard their own adult development as well.

Harry was a very competent and successful chief executive, a pillar of his church and community. He was ably assisted at home by his wife, Agnes, who ran the household, raised their four children and assisted at Harry's social functions. What Agnes did for Harry at home, his secretarial staff did at the office. Harry was an affable and caring man. It was easy to want to support him.

Agnes' sudden death pulled the rug out from under him. He was not only devastated, it seemed that his confidence had left him as well. At the office, his secretary could patch things over, cover for him when that was needed, but at home he was at a loss. Nannies and caretakers came and went. He shrunk from the idea of dating again. Who could ever replace Agnes?

His oldest child, Teresa, then fourteen, was entering her adolescence. It showed in the strange books she was reading and the swooning with friends about a matinee idol. She seemed a natural with her younger siblings: affectionate, yet firm when needed, and organized. They cleaved to her as the one who seemed to be there all the time. Teresa kind of lost interest in her romances and the movie star. Harry did not discourage Teresa from taking over the childcare and she did not seem to mind either. It settled his restlessness, his bewilderment as to how to cope by himself with his four kids. As time passed, he started to turn to Teresa to settle disputes between the kids, to come up with ideas about what to do on the weekends, plan meals, interview a new caretaker. By then his daughter had become a substitute mother for her own brothers and sister.

Harry never remarried. For the world he was still the epitome of a successful manager; little did the world know how he relied more and more on the devotion of his secretary. As he got older, he became increasingly self-absorbed and distant from his children.

Teresa evidently had skipped adolescence altogether. After seeing her siblings through their education and settled in their own lives, she remained to take care of her ailing father. After his death she worked for a charitable organization, and finally, got depressed.

With therapy, she realized that she had surrendered her youth to help her brothers and sister, propping up her father in the process. Her own development was the price she paid, unwittingly. She had not led a life of her own, even after her constant caring ended. She had lost sight of the need to balance care for others with care for oneself.

She did recover some territory. After taking a difficult art course, she became a well-known weaver of complex wall hangings, the kind that enlivens impersonal boardrooms.

Harry never got to see how much he depended on women for his success, or how his leaning on his daughter had stunted her growth, and had prevented him from trying out another way of coping as a widower, one that might have left him less dependent, more in charge of his life, more available to others, especially his children. Harry's late adulthood was not what it could have been.

After this caveat we may continue. The ways by which our children can contribute to our adult development remain open throughout our shared adult lives. As parents, we can continue to use their effect on us when we try to do what the parents did whom you have met so far in these pages. If we try to make a *summary of parental attitudes that foster child effects* it comes out somewhat like this:

The parents spent time with their children and got to know them well through all the transformations of childhood. Without knowing someone well, how can we begin to understand what they mean when they say or do something that is less then clear?

They did pay attention to the child's reaction to them, and to what they, as parents, were doing or saying. Some of these reactions were minimal: a change in behavior, a gesture, a facial expression. Sometimes they were clear: a yelp, a comment, a withdrawal. All these symbols need to be interpreted. The better these parents knew their child (and themselves) the easier that interpretation came. They were attentive to the signals indicating that the kid was moving into a new stage in its development. When the child started a sequence, they picked up on it. This participation determined the outcome of their interaction for both of them.

They remained receptive and reflective. No matter how provocative the child could be, they avoided knee-jerk reactions. These shortcuts can backfire. They did not blow a fuse. They did try to think before they acted. They reflected on what the child could have meant. They listened with an inner ear to their own emotions as they were aroused. They let memories well up and percolate. They faced the music. They noticed that it was often precisely when they felt a little embarrassment, some reluctance to proceed, some pain even during this introspective process, that they knew the child's effect was on target; that it had touched an area they'd rather not look into. They knew then that they were trying to avoid some unfinished business. It took courage to face down this resistance. They were honest with themselves and knew, deep down, that in some way the child was right and trying to be helpful. Weaving back and forth between the child's reaction to them and their reaction to the child, they hit developmental pay dirt. They could arrive at a useful insight about themselves. They did not need to retaliate or ignore the child. In other words, they let the relationship speak for itself. It became more than just two people interacting. In this mirror held up to them, they could see themselves as the child saw them and ask, "Is that who I want to be?"

When they finally reacted, they had their homework done. The reaction of the child to this response showed them if they were on the right track. If they were not, they'd start all over, or try something else next time. If the reaction they settled on was different from what they used to be doing, the novelty of acting "out of character" would wear off. Then the positive feedback from the child, and the intuitive sense of "I am doing something that feels just right," led them to change, slowly, but surely, their style of doing things and their character. They had grown a bit each time.

Growing up this way becomes for parent and child not unlike a dance. Each learns to adapt to the movements of the other, even though one may be leading. Growing up this way can be joyful and rewarding for both.

Philippe Aries, who wrote the classic *Centuries of Childhood*, concludes that only in the 15th or 16th century can we find the child depicted on its own in art, although still dressed as an adult. Medieval society did not know the idea of childhood as a separate stage of life. Children were often humiliated before adolescence was discovered in the 18th century. From then on, adolescence expanded, encroaching upon childhood and maturity, and it seems to be the "privileged age" of the 20th century.

We know all too well that adolescence has no defined end. It is not getting any easier to assume the responsibilities of adult life.

I have limited the scope of this book to that period of adult life in which we raise our kids. After adolescence, we reach the stage during which we do not raise them anymore, or barely at all. Life and its experiences will take over from us. In this period, our grown children do continue to effect us in much the same ways we have now become somewhat familiar with. But then, so do many other people: spouses, friends, teachers, even strangers, or public figures we do not even know personally.

The only other period during which we will again be involved in raising children, albeit of a different kind, will be when we become grandparents. We will look at that interaction in a following chapter.

First I want to spend some time with parents who are raising a child that puts an undue burden on them and see how this affects them and their development.

CHAPTER SEVEN

THE UNDULY BURDENED PARENT: SPECIAL-NEEDS CHILDREN: THE "BAD FIT"

Mental illness is hereditary, you get it from your children.
Bumper sticker

Now we take a look at those family situations where parenthood may become a hazard for the growing adult. The normal strains associated with raising kids, of course, can rise to a pitch where our usual level-headedness snaps. We can have our adult tantrums. These occasional lapses of parental composure need not necessarily become a hazard to us or to our children, as the tongue-in-cheek exasperation of the bumper sticker seems to imply.

The outcome of these embarrassing interactions, be they short-lived or extended over time, can be balanced. On one scale we have the features associated with the parent, on the other, those pertaining to the child. What makes a parent so vulnerable to stress, beyond the occasional and acceptable drops in tolerance, that we can say that adult development is at risk? And what kind of children are, even for average parents, so burdensome to raise, that parenting becomes a liability for them?

There is a third condition for hazardous parenting in which neither parent nor child can be considered in any way to be very unusual or abnormal, but the combination of the two makes for a bad fit; a risky coalition that turns into a hazard for the parent's development as an adult.

We will look first at the category of the ill-prepared parent, then at the unusually burdensome child, and finally at the risky coalition.

The Ill-Prepared Parent

Is there any parent, especially a first-timer, who feels completely prepared for the task at hand? But just as some people are created more equal, there are some among us who are even less ready for this awesome task of preparing the next generation before we move to Florida. Who are these unfortunate people who have parenthood thrust on them without a fighting chance to make something good out of it and who end up short-changed? Who dares to judge parental readiness? If anyone would claim this wisdom…can you hear the outcry?

We all know some perfectly adjusted and mature people who have made a mess of their children, as well as some disadvantaged and flaky people who raise resourceful kids. I don't know of any valid criteria for parental fitness. This lack of criteria for parental fitness may be just one more price we pay for our freedoms.

Perhaps we can try to sketch some outer boundaries of a group of people for whom parenthood turns out to be an unprofitable challenge or even a traumatic experience. Not only their children will be traumatized by the experience of growing up, but they themselves are victimized as well, a point which is rarely addressed. They are truly victimized and their further progress on the path to old age has been rendered rockier.

In our society it is increasingly difficult for parents to do their parenting. The ability to procreate is insufficient preparation for today's parenthood. Those who appreciate this, delay parenthood and skip to the next hurdle. Those who don't, become teenage parents.

Many teenage parents, wed or unwed, are in no shape to bring up the next generation to be civil, responsible, contributing members of the human species. How could it be otherwise? Many of them have not yet attained that status themselves.

The teenage, pregnant, high school girl, or the father of the unborn child, may opt for an abortion or give the child up for adoption, and thereby avoid parenthood, and resume their life with minimal interruption. For Grace this scenario was not available.

Grace came from a background of poverty and a fundamentalist religion. At the age of nineteen, she wanted to escape her social and emotional limitations. Perhaps a child would be the answer to her prayers? A new status? A shortcut to adulthood? Who knows. The magic of the romance did not hold; before the baby came the father left. Her community censored her for wantonness and failed to support her. Her mother declined to take yet another child. Grace had been the last of five. She had had enough.

Grace kept the child and tried to raise it, alternating between self-sacrificial caring and embittered resentment and rage. Her chances for an education were compromised. Her emotional growth and social development in contact with peers and co-workers was curtailed. She stayed home with the child. Her need to draw strength from a dependable person was not stilled. How could she become dependable when she still was so dependent herself? Her child's needs threatened and annoyed her. She would either overindulge ("Mama will always take care of you!") or rage ("Just wait till you hear me scream!"). Not only was her sense of independence undeveloped, her autonomy could not take hold under these conditions, nor her skills in connecting with a community.

Instead of having escaped, Grace found herself trapped in

the same web as her mother: unstable, angry, rejecting of her child, poor and bitter; her chances for finding a partner reduced. Parenthood was too flimsy a ticket to get to adulthood. She was ill-prepared, having and keeping the child victimized them both. Her adult development would have to be a makeshift affair with the outcome in serious doubt.

One does not have to be a teenager to be emotionally or psychologically ill-prepared to be a parent just yet. Parenthood can be thrown upon someone who is unprepared to assume its responsibilities. In that case parenthood suddenly lays bare some limitations which make one vulnerable to suffer from the process of raising children. Responsibility and power belong together. Power without responsibility is a prescription for disaster. It can be extremely traumatic to have responsibility thrust upon us before we have the power to act responsibly. Responsibility without power, "before one's time," makes us feel foolish and guilty for not having acted responsibly. Shame, guilt and powerlessness are a toxic cocktail if there ever was one! Take the story of Timothy.

Tim was fourteen years old when his mother jumped on a motorcycle and, following her bliss, roared to a post-sixties commune in the West. She had been, to some extent, understandably fed up with her workaholic, doctor husband who had assigned her, a freshly liberated woman, to the home and an ever-increasing brood. Her own strict and dutiful upbringing did little for her: belatedly; she rebelled.

Tim, the oldest of three kids, kind of fell into the vacated role. He valiantly tried to be mother and father to his siblings. Father was no big help. Besides his work, he was taken up by courting a new mate. Who wants three kids in one swoop?

At forty-one, Tim, a successful architect, renowned as a good organizer of big projects, came for help. Unfortunately, his relationships with women were shot through with frustration. He had left his wife and mother of his only child. "She was so independent." His affair with a boisterous, vibrant actress was just that. Bereft from sustaining company, feeling helpless to deal with the imminent departure of his oldest child for boarding school, he had finally become depressed.

Tim had learned not to ask for help during his premature recruitment into adulthood. As a pseudo-parent, he had repeatedly knocked for help on doors that remained closed: Father, relatives, officials. He tried to raise his siblings, relying for the real-life power on the distant father and his own wits. This "parenthood," these "children." made him skip whole chapters from the book of adolescence: play, explorations of intimacy, trials and errors in trust, limits of a growing competence, and living within limits. Finding out who he was, what he could do by himself and what he needed help with, was all put on hold.

His life was dominated by duty; its fruit was the fear of wanting to chuck it all (as his mother had done). Guilt for any slack in his conscientiousness drove him on (like his father). Later events in his life that required growth (separation from his child) gave him pause and a chance to reconsider it all.

Besides the immature (Grace) or premature (Tim) parent, there is yet another category of parent that is ill prepared. We are talking about people whose personal problems are such that they interfere with competent as well as gainful parenting. These people have to run an obstacle course with hurdles while one leg is in a cast. Of course they fall, get injured more, and have to get up again and get on with it.

In this group we see mothers and fathers for whom the defensive maneuver of limiting the child-effects to signals alone is not enough. Living with and having to care for children interferes with the evolution of their own adulthood.

To meet the non-negotiable needs of the child, they would have to adjust more than their limitations allow. These parents cannot adequately meet the needs for sustained nurturing, affection, encouragement or consistent limit setting. On account of this, the child can develop into its own variety of "difficult child," thereby escalating the demands for parental skills. The daily confrontation with such a growing child becomes a variety of the ancient Chinese water torture.

I will give one example of a personality type to illustrate this kind of ill-prepared parent. Having to raise children is a handicap to the maturation of these people.

Gloria was a handsome woman. She seemed to have it all: a keen mind, sporty tastes, a flair for dressing. She drew all eyes to her. Married to a wealthy banker who doted on her and whose home she enlivened, she seemed to thrive.

She had to be the focus of attention. With many admirers, she had precious few good friends. She was a self-absorbed person, completely caught in the contemplation of her own image as reflected by others—just like the mythological youth who was so absorbed by the reflection of his beauty in a pool that he drowned and turned into a narcissus.

Her limitations were visible in her children and how she dealt with them. She had bold ideas of how and what they should be. They had to be active, good sports, popular and above all, not make a fuss. "Stop crying! What are you, a wimp?" would be her response to the child who fell off the pony and hesitated to go back on. Empathy with someone else's feelings was just too difficult for Gloria.

We all know people like Gloria. Many of us are somewhat like her. The problem with the Glorias of either gender is that they leave so little room for the loving or being loved by another person. Early on they seem to have lost the trail that leads from the "I" to the "thou;" the trail we all need to find in order to be able to be with and for someone else.

Too busy molding her children in her own image, she was not one to be able to benefit by their child-effects. Their questions, comments, early tentative voices of protest, challenge or criticism, were simply disregarded, discounted and discouraged. Gloria could not hear the truth from anyone, even from her own children.

Her adult life started with glamour and promise. During mid-life, however, Gloria became progressively isolated. She never understood why her husband left her in a powerless rage. Had she not contributed to his career and raised his kids? "Trained" might be a better word. She who was so ill-equipped for the most human of charges, believed she was actually accomplishing it! Gloria was tough and determined. She embarked defiantly on "a new life of my own," centered around her horses and a trendy boutique she had opened.

How, will you ask, were her kids in any way a hazard for her? By most standards she was a hazard for them and their growth. But from the viewpoint of the absence of child-effects, the hazard to her is less glaring, but no less real.

Gloria had made her offspring her project for the "best years of her life." She ran a tight ship, but not a caring, understanding one. She remained impervious to their reactions or comments that did not fit her scenario. Her kids had learned not to challenge her or hold a mirror up to her. Precisely because of this, she had been unreceptive to the child-effects as we have described them in Chapter One, and of the rewards from them.

Gloria came for help in late middle age. Nothing resembling wisdom was yet emerging. Even her interests in beautiful people and exotic tastes had not begun to encompass the future or life's larger questions. She had no inkling where her distress came from; her bitterness and frustration. Gloria had been stagnating for twenty-five years.

The hazard the children presented to her was twofold. First, it was time spent without the benefit of input from them, their symbols and sequences were wasted on her. She had lacked the vitamin of their enabling influence on her adult development. Raising her kids was like window dressing an empty store. Second, this distracted her from seeing the emptiness of her life and love-poor relationships.

Like the evil queen in *Snow White*, Gloria surrounded herself with mirrors reassuring her she was "the most beautiful in the land." Snow White, of course, is put into a long sleep until true love finally wakes her up. No child-effects will bring relief to these fundamentally lonely and hard to love people. Self-love remains barren.

Adults like Gloria stand a better chance for eventual development without their children, but this takes a long and arduous exploration. Such an enterprise can lead to less of a focus on the self, provided it is done under experienced guidance with a trained and knowledgeable therapist. Under these conditions a more fulfilling, though perhaps less colorful, life can yet emerge.

The Abusive Parent

The abusive parent is another ill-equipped parent who tries to raise children and can be hamstrung in their adult development. The daily requirement of having to care for, to discipline, to listen to, to encourage and give of oneself, is painfully difficult for the person who still feels that he or she did not receive enough in their own childhood or were not encouraged, listened to and cared for. It's just very hard to be generous when we still feel empty and angry inside.

Clinical experience and research has shown that the abusive

parent frequently is an abused child grown old, but not up. Those who were not loved, love with great difficulty. The daily confrontation with the escalating demands and needs of the children raises feelings of helplessness and rage in these deprived parents. They experienced these same feelings during their own abuse as children, as passive victims. As adults and parents, this helpless passivity avenges itself in their actions of an unloving, abusive kind, and victimizes the helpless child.

Even if these actions do not produce feelings of guilt, certainly they do not contribute to a resolution of the parents' past trauma and a freeing up of his potential for increased self-esteem and competence as a parent. Not unlike Gloria, they remain locked in a chain of misery that spans generations of victims and victimizers. The roles are reversed, but the pattern is maintained.

We find this often when alcoholism, chemical dependency, sexual exploitation or physical abuse is involved. The children, with their natural appeal for care, arouse in these parents old pains of an uncaring past. Again, the children become the unwitting obstacles to breaking the treadmill that they and their parents are trapped in, each losing chances for growth. Not until their children leave, sometimes not until they have grandchildren, are these parents able to pick up the lost opportunity to resume a life of their own.

THE UNUSUALLY BURDENSOME CHILD

Let us turn our attention to the other kind of hazards that children present to parental growth; the risks to normal parents of the unusually burdensome child. If parenthood becomes a burden on most parents some of the time, caring for an unusually burdensome child overloads any parent most of the time. This unusual stress requires extraordinary coping skills and supports.

We will look briefly at parents whose child has a serious

physical or mental handicap. These special burdens on families can affect the normal development of the parents.

In these families there is no "life as usual." Their expectations, hopes and activities, all have to accommodate this intrusive reality. The parent is challenged to come to terms with this double predicament. It should not surprise us that extraordinary outcomes of parental adult evolution are more the rule than the exception.

At first, Mary did not even mention that Brian, her brother, was brain-damaged and retarded. She came to me to find relief, as a grown-up woman, for a mild depression following the birth of her second child. Personally, she would rarely draw attention to herself. She lived in the shadow of her husband, a robust, successful, engineering professor. She was not assertive without being passive. She tended to avoid conflicts by deferring to others and to compromise. She had been a good student, well liked by many, and was happily and quietly married.

In passing, she had mentioned her younger brother who now was living in a protected setting. Exploring the role of this child in the family and its effect on the members, helped us understand not only how Mary had become so self-effacing, but also why her second child, reviving her old resentments about her own younger sibling, had triggered her depression. But let us listen to what she said about her parents:

"They really were totally devoted to Brian. They simply refused to let him go to an institution. The house was turned upside down to accommodate him and what he needed: precautions, special equipment, extra lessons and exercises, and a lot of attention. The best I could do was to get out of the way and lead my own life. I just didn't want to burden them any more with my little problems.

"It wasn't easy, especially for Mom, I think. Dad changed jobs and shifts so they could take turns at being with Brian. I know Mom went through bad years, wondering what went wrong to get Brian so messed up before he was even born. I guess she felt guilty about that. Dad would get angry whenever she talked like that or just cried. I even remember going to counseling sessions as a family. They cried and swore a lot. I shut up. Later I was told that they almost broke up at some point.

"Mom gave up a lot: her teaching job, her church activities, and her gardening. Brian became pretty much an obsession for them. I had school and my friends, but I did not always want to bring them home.

"Mom and Dad did go out, but people rarely visited us, not even family. Only later, when Brian got older and we moved to P., did they get help with him. Now, of course, he is thirty and lives in a shelter. I think Mom and Dad are only now picking up their own lives again."

This is not an unusual account. The literature of the effects of the handicapped children on their parents does not focus as much on the personal growth of the parent as it does on the nature of the trauma to the parent, their coping style, the psychological and social needs, and their mental health in general.[xl]

The presence of a handicapped child can totally change the focus of family life, away from each other and to only one needy individual and its survival. We do not abandon these unfortunates as other mammals do. For our devotion we pay a price. Each member gets less of what they want, need or expect. Husbands will find their wives less available; kids get less from their parents; and wives from being a mother and from the world outside the house.

Life is revealed as unfair and fate as capricious. Why our child? Why us? How can we fit this into a sustaining worldview, or live with this burden and survive as a functioning family? It leaves its mark not only on children like Mary, but also on parents: on their evolving self-image and on the maintenance of the reciprocal give-and-take, which allows us to count our blessings as we pour balm on each other's bruises. Lastly, it is a major challenge to the formation of an outlook on life, which is needed for integrity in old age.

Occasionally we hear very different outcomes. Here the unusually burdensome child brings out unexpected resources in the parents or their communities. The result can be, after all is said and done, quite positive. The fabric of the family is preserved and strengthened as each member contributes to the common task and yet preserves time for the others. The integrity of the parents can be fortified—a not uncommon result of weathering a serious storm.

A family that holds together this way can make a claim for having gained by keeping the disabled child in their midst. They tell us about human resilience and about the conditions that make such a positive outcome possible.

The Pantulis chose to keep their daughter after it became apparent that she had a brain disorder that would impair her development and interfere with theirs.

The Pantulis married late in life. Both were independent, highly trained and successful entrepreneurs. They specialized in making marginal companies become more productive. Their life and business was intertwined. They loved it and wanted a child. Noelle was born: a delightful baby, lovely and cute. The felt that life's abundance was theirs for the picking.

Soon, however, it became apparent that Noelle was not growing as she should. She also needed increasingly more care. She was examined and the Pantulis were told she would never be a normal child. After two years of growing frustration, the couple got in each other's way and almost gave up their child and the marriage. Defeat? That was not in their vocabulary. It didn't help that the father's parents argued for giving up Noelle. They were proud, perfectionist and demanding people. They wouldn't want their son to be identified as the father of an invalid child. Resentful of this interference, Mr. Pantuli learned to help care for his little daughter and the couple went for marital therapy. With a new understanding of their life together, they decided to take on Noelle's challenge.

Schedules and routines were rearranged. They found a support group for mothers of disabled children. Social agencies were tapped for their resources. As Noelle grew up, their marriage held up and even improved. Each discovered hidden aspects of themselves. Mr. Pantuli wrested a new identity away from what he was supposed to be: the golden son; the bearer of fame and pride. He became a dedicated father of an invalid child. Mrs. Pantuli discovered that she could actually depend on others for sustenance: on her husband for Noelle's care, on the support of the other mothers and the social agencies.

Noelle remained a sweet kid who charmed all that met her. At age seventeen, her size and vulnerability finally convinced her parents that she would be better off in a residential facility. Noelle had received a loving start in life and managed the transition well.

These parents commented on how keeping their daughter had turned their lives around. The father became aware of becoming independent of his parents' expectations and their manipulation of him, as well as of his more modest version of himself. He no longer had a "can do all, and succeed in anything" cockiness. He was now a little embarrassed about it.

The mother marveled at how she had allowed herself to become dependent, enjoying this in her many new friendships. She too, felt humbled by the experience as well as enriched by it.

Both realized the conditions that made this survival possible: their high motivation and resourcefulness, and the support from counselors, friends and social agencies. With these kinds of supports, the "burdensome child" may occasionally be a blessing in disguise. Both deeply religious people, the Pantulis remarked that God had given them a much needed chance to turn their lives around. "Nothing else would have been able to do that but Noelle."

Accounts like this one seem to find their way into upbeat or inspirational literature. The search for meaning leads to a spiritual dimension that transforms the whole experience into something more than only a burden carried well.

For most parents of unusually burdensome children, the way ahead will lay somewhere in between the extremes of the examples given here. We find a mix of the tragic and the uplifting. The effect of the child on the parent also becomes a blend of the troublesome effects and the positive contributions to their personality development.

We now come to the last category of negative child-effects on the parent: where parent and child are mismatched.

The Risky Coalition

The concept of a "bad fit" between two individuals so closely related, so intimately connected as parent and child, is not an easy one to entertain nor a popular one to hold. We leave aside the comments made in desperation or anger whenever the going gets tough in the family. "I really don't understand you! You're so different! Am I a foundling? Are you sure you're my Mom?" We do not seriously want to consider a bad fit as being beyond our ability to fix.

Yet this same notion of irreconcilable differences is invoked in other intimate relationships. "But," you'll say rightly, "there we choose, or so it seems. We do not choose our children, nor they us!" If we allow children their own temperaments, style and personalities, even from very early on, why should we be surprised that now and then a child is so fundamentally different from a parent that even the parental bonding and the best of intentions and patience are all of no avail to bridge that gap. The "otherness" of the child is too radical. It overshadows the common aspects. The connection is never really made.

The least bad fate of such a parent is not to be able to gain the full benefit from child-effects. The worst is of alienation from this "stranger." We find a classic example of the latter kind of bad fit in the novel of Ivan Turgenyev: *Fathers and Sons.*[xli]

In his novel, Turgenyev gives us two sets of father-son relationships: Arkady, Bazarov and their fathers. Arkady's parents are from the landed gentry. They are trying to follow their son's maturing as a young adult who is under the influence of the social changes taking place in pre-Revolutionary Russia. They have their ups and downs. At one point, Arkady exclaims: "A son cannot judge his father, least of all I, and least of all such a father who, like you, has never hampered my liberty in any way!"

Next to Arkady we get to know his best friend, Bazarov, a contrast in nature if ever there was one. Bazarov is aloof, intellectual, revolutionary and seemingly unfeeling until he falls in love. Arkady is at first swept up by his friend's austere and radical ideas, but distances himself from them gradually as he, too, falls in love. He turns to a family-oriented life.

Bazarov's parents are humble country folk who try as best they can to understand their son, the young doctor, whose attitude and ideas baffle them. After a long absence, Bazarov finally visits them, at Arkady's urging. They are mystified by his seeming rejection of them. But their love prevails over his rudeness and, when Bazarov gets infected during an operation on a seriously ill peasant and dies at home, the description of their grief has few equals in literature.

The alienation from their son left these parents in rural simplicity, unable to even connect with this revolutionary visitor. Only their faith sustained them, and we are left wondering if their isolation was their salvation, while Bazarov died a godless death. One could say that here the bad fit seems to have protected the parents from their son's influence. Superficially this may be true. His rationalistic ideals were an insurmountable obstacle. His character was too unlike theirs. But a human, personal, relationship was absent and they remained essentially unchanged, in utter stagnation.

In a similar situation, the outcome for parents can be less benign.

Oscar was the last of four children born to a poor, Latvian immigrant family. Their home was in one of the poorest sections of a large city. Life was grubby and the struggle for life was unceasing. Even as a child, Oscar looked and acted differently. He was fine-boned with an angelic face. His brothers were rough-hewn and robust. Of course he was singled out for taunts and jokes, innuendoes in school and on the street. At home, his parents were at a loss to understand his interests: books, school and religion. His father, perhaps threatened by his son's perceived "lack of manliness," at first tried to toughen him up by taking him to ball games and boxing, but, not seeing any results, gave up and withdrew with barely concealed contempt. His mother was preoccupied with his two rowdy older siblings, the "real boys" and the sister. Since Oscar was such a good boy, she could leave him pretty much alone in his room

He describes his youth as bleak, lonely, and "like being in a foreign country, not even speaking the same language." Oscar found some support and a chance to emancipate himself in the studio of a local artist. He was encouraged by this new friend and a few of his teachers who took a liking to him, and began to make his own way in his own world: the artistic community.

Later he sought psychiatric help because of a strong self-defeating tendency. It was clear that he felt guilt for having abandoned his family. His success as an artist widened the gulf between their slovenly misery and his increasing affluence and status. He became a well-known silversmith. On his sporadic visits home, he tried to establish a contact across a chasm between two different styles and experiences. "They do not even know what questions to ask," he says ruefully.

They never learned to. As Oscar soared in his art, married and became a parent himself, his parents remained what they had been: unable to profit from any of his potential contributions to their lives. Theirs was a different world altogether.

We can easily find cases of a bad fit when a sudden eruption of a talent sets the gifted child apart from his environment. This may lead to attempts to make it conform, or to an early recognition of the difference and an attempt to enlarge the scope of parental care with another understanding adult.

But what happens if parents try to bring up this alien creature by themselves? Oscar's parents had other kids they could identify with. They got along in the way these families get along, but Oscar remembers his father's bewilderment and contempt for "this sissy, my boy," and recalls his mother's puzzlement and how she avoided him.

What if Oscar had been an only child? The "otherness" we parents need for our harvest of child-effects can be so extreme that it becomes like living with a familiar stranger, not ever really connecting. The rewards and reinforcements of parenthood are denied and parents can end up feeling inadequate, instead of affirmed by the child. Parents of a freak; freak parents.

What else can parents do besides trying to raise the "odd one out?" They can reject the child. This is a self-preserving effort, which has its own dangers for the development of parental identity. The further unfolding of the personality into more generative and integrative phases will be in jeopardy.

The extreme examples lead us to geniuses that we know or human wrecks we ignore, and the middle ground is littered with compromises. There is naturally some "mismatching" going on even in regular families, where the degree of "otherness" is a challenge to parental pride and a source of diversity for the tribe. Where parental pride is high or where extreme differences prevail, we can see the damage done to their development as well as to that of the growing, unusually different, child.

CHAPTER EIGHT

GRANDPARENTS AND GRANDCHILDREN:
ACROSS THE GENERATIONS

"Grow old along with me
the best is yet to be
the last of life for which
the first was made"
Robert Browning

As a small boy one of my favorite stories was *Little Lord Fauntleroy*, the popular children's work by Frances Hodgson Barnett. It tells the story of Cedric Errol, who, at the age of seven, upon becoming the heir to his English grandfather's title, travels to England with his widowed American mother. Eventually the small boy's sincerity and winning ways reconcile his crusty old grandfather to his commoner daughter-in-law (Cedric's mother). Written in 1886, and well illustrated, the story enjoyed worldwide popularity despite its unleavened sentimentality. Yet something of the story's original appeal for me still persists. Children do inspire transformations across generations.

Charles Dickens was something of a specialist in this area. What reader can ever forget Macwith, the terrifying escaped convict of *Great Expectations*, transformed by only two encounters with Dickens' young narrator, Pip? Or Ebenezer Scrooge, the most notorious miser since Shylock, who abandons his skinflint ways after witnessing Tiny Tim's cheerful acceptance of his handicap. A recent example can be found in Alvin Rosenfeld's *A Dissenter in the House of God,* a novel about a Holocaust survivor whose numbed emotional life is gradually thawed out by a young apprentice who reminds him of his dead son.

Whatever their literary merits, I believe that part of what attracts us to these stories is their insight that children can exert a benign influence on adults, even two generations removed. And why not? If child-effects can help parents, there is no reason why grandparents, who share a special relationship with their grandchildren, can't benefit as well, and get, as it were, a second helping of the rewards of parenthood.

This raises two questions: What direction do we want to grow in for our late adulthood? And: How can our grandchildren help us with this?

DIFFERENCES BETWEEN MIDDLE AND LATE ADULTHOOD

Another way of framing the first questions would be: What do we hope to see in our elders, if we still want to rely on them? To find an answer, we only have to look at what seems to be a rule of developmental steps: the needs of the younger generation seemto outline the developmental requirements of the older one, in much the same way a template forms its imprint. For example, as children we are best served if our parents have learned to establish and maintain intimate relationships, are mature enough to commit themselves to the nurture and support of the family, and have disciplined themselves to advancement in a chosen career rather than scattering their energies and talents with no thought for the future.

The young set the agenda for the older generation's development. What do they need us to be when we are about to enter the last stages of our personal growth? How do they help us to become that way?

I found my own answer to that question in 1986, while attending the American Psychiatric Convention. These annual gatherings feature at least one special lecture by a highly respected guest, not necessarily from our own field. That year Argentinean writer Jorge Luis Borges was invited. Well into his eighties, Borges was a striking man. His powers, including the ability to quote extensively from world literature, seemed undiminished by his blindness or age. His soft, melodious voice held us in thrall.

Listening to him, and seeing the transfixed expressions of my fellow psychiatrists, moved me greatly. Here was a capacity audience of learned men and women, almost all younger than the speaker, listening to this archetypal sage: the blind seer. Stripped of the incidentals of Borges' presence and his incantatory presentation, the content of his message was not groundbreaking. No matter. The messenger was himself the embodiment of truth, at least as important as anything he might have said. Our culture may be obsessed with youth, but when we are presented with an articulate example of a long life come to fruition we are moved to reverence.

Borges and my fellow psychiatrists were re-enacting an ancient tribal ceremony: he was the wise old man whose status was safeguarded by our esteem; we could seek his counsel without shame. We could applaud what we might have dismissed if it had come from, let's say, a thirty-five-year-old junior faculty member.

Borges epitomized what we look for in the elders of our tribe. We saw in him what all of us needed: wisdom, respect for tradition, a non-polemical perspective, and an inspiring example.

Wisdom, that distillation of lived experience; the integration of passion and patience, imagination and knowledge, comes, if at all, as the prize of old age.

Allied with wisdom is a sense of continuity, especially in an age that values novelty for its own sake. The elders, and all before them, grappled with the same questions of life as we do. We want our elders to be the guardians of tradition.

Thirdly, elders offer us a perspective that rises above the fray. Turf battles and internal conflicts have to be settled before late adulthood. The elder statesman is not partisan; the matriarch chooses no sides. Personal conflicting interests and impulses need to be reconciled before we can speak of *integrity*. From their unique vantage point of beginning detachment, they can offer us a transcending vision.

Lastly, the elders, already within sight of death, continue to lead the way. Even as they age and become infirm we would like them to exemplify how the final acts of life can still be dignified, so that our fears may be allayed. With the immanence of death, we want them to point to the transcendence of life.

This is quite a fancy wish list! Is it one of life's unattainable fantasies? The wish for the ideal parent? Let us back off and say that the above description points to a potential, not to a standard. Nevertheless, examples of people who attain this level of development abound, if we only keep our eyes open and look for them. We ignore their example at our peril.

If the above begins to answer the first part of our question (what direction do we want to grow in for our late adulthood?) we now turn to the second part: How can our grandchildren help us with this? Isn't that asking too much of the younger generation?

The following vignette illustrates how one elderly man became a remarkable grandfather through the intervention of his children and the effects of his grandchildren.

Earl was a retired clergyman. He belonged to the generation whose children were raised by their mothers. Fatherhood was limited to the role of provider and protector. "Fathering" didn't begin until children reached grade school. His daughters rarely saw him, except in the evening before going to bed, and even then they had to compete for attention with their mother and the parents' social schedule.

Consequently, the birth of Earl's first grandchild propelled him totally unprepared into grandfatherhood. His apprehension was plain in the stiff-armed way he held the baby, but he put on a brave front, allowing his daughter Julie and her husband to coach him in the intricacies of burping and diapers. His attempts at purchasing appropriate books and toys were equally awkward, but improved with practice. At first the joy and pride he felt was largely ceremonial, but as his skills as a "hands-on" grandpa improved, he began to relish his competence in his new role.

Julie suggested that he had a new function in their lives, a dynastic one, with its own duties and responsibilities, which did not include childrearing. He could, for example, begin to share memories and heirlooms with his grandchildren, unique stories attached to the gifts only a grandfather can give. A born raconteur, Earl could become the family storyteller.

Earl took his daughter's advice. He was actually relieved that nobody expected him to be his grandchildren's disciplinarian. With his new role clearly defined, what he could do with his grandchildren and what he should give them, became less of a problem. So he wrote a lovely children's book for his youngest grandchild. Then his son-in-law asked him, as the oldest living repository of family lore, to write a family chronicle. With this coaching and appreciation, he gradually became a model grandfather. The grandchildren loved and respected him for his attachment to tradition. Grandpa could always be counted on to dress for dinner. As they grew into adulthood, he became even more fascinating for the perspective he provided on a way of life so different from their own.

Earl became the driving force behind annual gatherings of the whole family. His last project was an attempt to set down for the younger generations a summary of his views on life and how he had managed to live and age so well. Shortly after this, he fell seriously ill and after several days in the hospital, resigned himself to give up the struggle. But his children reminded him of how important he still was to them. Later, he credited his recovery to this assurance that he was still too needed to simply go.

This grandfather was made, not born. All three types of child-effects came into play. His perplexity at being promoted to grandfather (a signal), motivated him to learn some early parenting. His dynastic role set the tone for integration. Later, his accepting of different child-rearing methods (a symbol) loosened him enough to assume the expanded role of family patriarch. These changes opened the way for sequences; the frequent give-and-take between Earl and his grandchildren as both kept on growing. His old age, which might otherwise have been more static, now became an enriching period of his life and an inspiring example of maturation for others.

We see in this example how grandchildren can contribute to our growth in late life. What makes this so natural? To begin with, grandparents have more free time than the grandchild's parents do. They have the leisure to focus on essentials. Parents can be too distracted by other concerns to become involved in the child, or too tempted to use such small interludes for instruction or correction. Since most grandparents are not directly responsible for the care of the grandchildren, they can approach them more on the child's terms and less as a pre-figuration of what they believe the grandchild should become. Furthermore, the child can simply be with this adult in a non-demanding atmosphere. It can relax and enjoy this presence in its life. Reading stories together, admiring a flower or fixing a broken toy; the generations transcend their differences. Trust and closeness follow, priming their relationship for the most profitable of all child influences: sequences.

Grandchildren present us with our third chance to rework some old problems and reformulate late-life challenges. We need this if we aim for generativity and integration.

During a recent conversation the mother of a fifteen-month-old son made an interesting observation to me: "It's strange," she said, "For as long as I can remember, my father was a prickly old crock. There was only one way to do things: his way, and one opinion that was worthwhile: his opinion. In dinner-table conversations, he never allowed me or my brother to hold a viewpoint that contradicted his own, even if it meant simply shouting us down. After a while we just gave up trying to have any serious conversation with him, a situation that continues to this day. But our son David simply adores him. Whenever we visit my parents, he toddles right up to my father. It is awesome watching the two of them play together—there is none of the "do this or do that" that characterized the way my father "played" with us. With David, he seems completely different. He allows him to take the lead, even though he still can't talk to my brothers or me without becoming the boss again."

We have already seen how child-effects can alter the dynamics of an entire family instead of just one or two family members. Grandchildren can cause significant shifts in relations between grandparents and parents (see also Patty and Rick, Chapter Three). This can come about simply when the grandchildren's presence acts as a signal, or because of the grandchildren's interactions with their seniors, provoking symbols or sequences. Let me illustrate the latter first.

Amy, a young mother in therapy, described how her mother, Lilian, seemed to fear losing her grandchildren's affection. A failure to pay attention to her during her visits or any indication that her grandchildren disagreed with her, no matter how trifling, was seen by Lilian as a harbinger of rejection and earned sharp rebuke. The startled grandchildren soon withdrew from her thereby, of course, fulfilling Lilian's fears.

In describing these incidents, Amy began to recall her own difficulty as a child facing the emotional demands of an insecure mother. Over time, as she reconstructed this period from an adult perspective, she came to understand and actually to mollify some of her defensiveness in her relationship with her mother.

Lilian remained caught up in her problems with self-worth and dependence. She repeated with her grandchildren the difficulties she had experienced with her own children. Given her temperament and age, it was unlikely that Lilian would change. Still, there is always hope. Could it be that Lilian's discomfort with Amy as a child, now repeated with her grandchildren, on whom she was less dependent for affirmation, would prompt a different outcome this time?

It was interesting to see how watching her children's interactions with her mother provoked memories in Amy (my patient). Although Lilian did not change very much, Amy experienced a beneficial transformation. Understanding some of her mother's insecurities allowed her to put to rest some of her resentment at her mother's early behavior. While their relationship was far from ideal, Amy' mildness during her mother's infrequent visits has allowed moments of real caring to surface, something which had rarely before happened.

Reading about these grandparents' stories, we tend to overlook the fact that what we are looking at is the real effect children can have on older people, two generations removed. They do not need to be blood relatives, just as children can exert their formative influence on adults who are not their parents. We all know of the single teacher, social worker, or coach, whose development is kept going thanks to their involvement with youngsters. They make the gains of (grand)parenthood available to those elderly who are not real family relations.

Let us take as an example Mike, who was the "father" of Kate.

I met Mike when Kate, the twelve-year-old daughter of his wife from an earlier marriage, was referred to me for a minor learning disability. Mike was then about sixty-four. I was struck by her ease at relating to an older stranger. She was comfortable and unselfconscious. During my talk with them, the father treated her as equal, deferring to her when she seemed better informed, seeking her opinion when a question concerned her, aware and respectful when he had to decide for her. There was camaraderie between them, not a hierarchy. Kate could easily have been his grandchild. "I was fifty-two when Kate was born," he said, answering my unasked question.

His was an unusual story. He had come from an abusive family. His violent father ruled the roost with a leather strap. Mike left the farm as soon as he could, and became a drifter. In his twenties, he discovered a talent for painting and settled long enough to put himself through art school. While in the merchant marine, he won his first of many prizes. By then he was in his fifties. It was time to get married. Soon he found Candy, an art student thirty years his junior, with a child. Candy's scandalized family ("A painter you said? My God, he's bohemian! How old did you say he was?") was soon won over by Mike's unpretentiousness and deep affection for their daughter.

Mike's personal life continued with commissions, shows,

and friends visiting their rustic home in the hills of Connecticut. He took care of Kate when Candy was working in the nearby inn, and took her wherever he went: hiking, painting, or hunting. He went with her to 4H club events, and played softball with her and her friends in the yard. He had integrated his self-reliance with a desire to connect with the world. It was immaterial to him that he was approaching seventy.

Candy and Kate had come into his life at a time when patterns of living can become either entrenched or creatively rearranged. These two younger companions kept him limber and focused on the future. He responded to their constant challenges for change. Life for him was a renewable resource, not a shrinking commodity. There is little doubt in my mind that his life would have been more restricted had he devoted himself only to his art. Candy and Kate kept stirring the pot and he was willing to keep tasting from it.

Here an adult growth pattern, even aging, led to the full development of both generativity and integration at the same time, and not sequentially. The full fruition of an artistic talent and a rich family life came at the time that a life of self-reliance culminated in an affirmation of connection to other people.

Most of us have to content ourselves with carrying our lives out into the world and into the next generations through our flesh-and-blood offspring or through an occasional artistic creation. But the admirable examples of aging in this chapter have turned their very lives into works of art with the aid of grandchildren. They inspire us. They bear witness to a grace and dignity that we want to emulate.

The old and the young need each other. Their relationship nurtures both generations. The older person's instinctive attraction to vitality at a time of ebbing life may be matched with the younger person's need for a mentor or contact with a person of broader life experience. As grandparents know, contact with youngsters keeps them mentally, emotionally and often physically supple. Living in proximity to people of all ages has been found to increase general health and *decrease* mortality for older people, especially if relatives are nearby. Housing for the elderly is located preferably in the bustle of a populated area, not in a quiet backwater.

Whenever I hear people talking about what a burden old age is, I think of Borges, Earl and Mike. And when they are surprised at the bonding between kids and their grandparents, I think of the examples of redeeming child-effects on the development of their grandparents, which are the true rewards of grandparent-hood

End Notes

1 The term "gender equality" is associated with "political correctness." The genders are not quite equal, but equal value ought to be assigned to each.

i (i) *Newsweek* (May 4, 1991): 30.

ii (ii) *Juvenal* (Decimus Junius Juvenalis, Roman moralist and satirist, ca 55-127 CE).

iii (v) Carl Gustav Jung, Modern Man in Search of a Soul. Harcourt, Brace & Co. N.Y. 1933

iv (vi) Erik H. Erikson, Dimensions of a New Identity, Jefferson Lectures (New York; W. W. Norton, 1973)

v (vii) William Shakespeare, As You Like It, 2.7.142-166 (emphasis added).

vi (ix) Winifred Galagher. Midlife Myths. Atlantic Monthly, May 1993

vii (xi) Edward Forster (1879-1970), British novelist and essayist.

viii (xiii) Marcel Proust (1871-1922), A la Recherche du Temps Perdu, Gallimard, Paris, 1954.

ix (xiii) Erik H. Erikson, *The Lifestyle Completed* (New York, W.W. Norton, 1982).

x (xvi) George E. Vaillant and Eva Milofsky, "Natural History of Male Psychological Health," *American Journal of Psychiatry*, 137:11 (Nov. 1980).

xi (xvii) Daniel J. Levinson, The Seasons of a Man's Life. Alfred Knoff, New York. 1978

xii (xviii) Roger L. Gould, Transformations, Simon & Schuster, New York. 1978.

xiii (xix) Sir Francis Bacon (1561-1626) British statesman and philosopher. The Essays (1625), "Of Youth and Age" Peter

Pauper Press, Mt Vernon Press, New York. (no date given, nor relevent, I think

xiv Carol Gilligan, In a Different Voice, Harvard Iniv. Press, Cambridge, 1982

xv (xxi) J . E . Anthony and T. Benedek, Parenthood: Its Psychology and Psychopathology, Little, Brown. Boston, 1970

xvi (xxii) New York Times, April 14, 1988, section 3, p. 8.

xvii (xxiii) Ellen Galinski, The Six Stages of Parenthood, Addison-Wesley, Reading,MA, 1987

xviii (xxiv) Nancy Friday, My Mother/My Self, Dell, New York, 1977

xix (xxv) Dr Spock's book contains some valuable advice, Dr Brazelton is more contemporary. Dr Leache's is encyclopedic. Critical reading is best.

xx (xxvi) Jerome Kagan, Harvard Gazette, Sept 22, 1989

xxi (xxvii) Herbert Kohl, Growing with your Children, Little, Brown. Boston, 1978.

xxii (xxviii) William Trevor, Deadly Sins, "Gluttony", William Morrow & Co, New York, 1993

xxiii (xxix) Camillo Sbarbaro," Even If You Weren' My Father" , trans. Shirley Hazzard, The New Yorker, Aug 6, 1991

xxiv (xxx) see xiv .

xxv (xxxi) Jean Piaget et al . , The moral judgement of the child, trans . Marjorie Gabain, Free Press 1965

xxvi (xxxii) Eugene Peterson, "Eat This Book: The Holy Community at Table with Holy Scripture" , Theology Today, April 1999

xxvii (xxxiii) Agesilaus II, King of Sparta (444-630 BCE), famous for his statecraft and battles in that Kingdom's period of glory. Anecdote from: Johannes Pauli; "Schimpf und Ernst", Herbert Stubenrauch (Berlin, Verlagsbuchhandlung, 1924.

xxviii (xxxiv) Bruno Bettelheim, *A Good Enough Parent; a Book on Childrearing*, (New York, Alfred A. Knopf, 1987).

xxix (xxxv) Jean de la Bruyere, (1645-1696) , French Satiric moralist, Les Characteres, Audin, Paris, 1949.

xxx (xxxvi) Diane Casselberry Manuel, "Interview with Martina Horner," *Christian Science Monitor*, 12 April, 1984

xxxi (xxxvii) Johann Wolfgang von Goethe (1749-1932), Viking Book of Aphorisms, W. H. Auden e. a. Viking Press , 1991

xxxii Ralph Keyes ed., *Sons on Fathers*,(New York, HarperCollins, 1992).

xxxiii (xxxix) Robert Coles, *The Moral Intelligence of Children*, (New York, Random House, 1997).

xxxiv (xl) Ellen Goodman, "When the Moral Life of Children Jabs at Adults", Boston Globe, Oct 17, 1989

xxxv (xli) "A Conversation with Robert Coles," *Harvard Gazette*, 25 January, 1991.

xxxvi (xlii) D. Offer et al. "Adoloscence, What is Normal?", Yearbook of Psychiatry and Applied Mental Health, Mosby, Boston, 1991.

xxxvii (xliii) George E. Vaillant, *Adaptation to Life*, (Boston, Little, Brown, 1977).

xxxviii (xliv) Helen Meyers, "The Impact of Teenage Children on Parents", in: Middle Years, ed, John M. Oldman, Yale Univ. Press, New Haven, 1989.

xxxix (xlv) Doris Lessing, The Temptation of Jack Orkney and Other Stories, Alfred A. Knopf, New York, 1973.

xl (xlv) Mary Murphy. PH.D. The family with a handicapped child, a review of the litterature. Devel. and Behav.
Pediatrics, 3.2. . , pg 73-82 June 1982.

xli (xlvi) Ivan S. Turgenyef, (1818-1883), Fathers and Sons, trans. Guilbert Guerney, Modern Library, 1961.